SHORT BIKE RIDES ON LONG ISLAND

THIRD EDITION

by
Phil Angelillo

An East Woods Book

The Globe Pequot Press

Old Saybrook, Connecticut

Copyright © 1977, 1983, 1989, by Phil Angelillo

Short Bike Rides is a trademark of the Globe Pequot Press, Inc.

Angelillo, Phil.

Short bike rides on Long Island / Phil Angelillo. - 3rd ed.
"An East Wood Book."
p. cm.
ISBN 0-87106-636-X
1. Bicycle touring - New York (State) - Long Island - Guide-
books   2. Long Island (N.Y.) - Description and travel -
Guide-books.   I. Title
GV1045.5.N72L663   1989
917.47'21-dc20

                                                    89-33739
                                                        CIP

Manufactured in the United States of America
Third Edition/Fourth Printing

About the Author

Phil Angelillo is a native New Yorker who, for more than twenty-five years, has enjoyed the unique pleasures of bicycling in the metropolitan area. Of particular interest to him are the varied neighborhoods' lifestyles and histories. With his wife and two sons he has traveled almost every road on Long Island and has thus gained a deep appreciation of its myriad attractions. In addition to his bicycling activities, Mr. Angelillo enjoys remodeling a waterside home on Long Island Sound, along with walking and rowing its shores.

Table of Contents

Introduction

Long Island is a cyclist's delight. Its contrasting environments, long history, and varied social makeup provide a kaleidoscope of attractions and scenery, all of it on generally easy bicycling terrain. This book presents thirty rides that explore the areas of Long Island that best display its essential character and unique historical and geographic features. They span the island from the New York City border to the easternmost tips of its flukes, along flat Atlantic Ocean seashore, wooded hills on the Long Island Sound shore, bountiful farms, picturesque villages steeped in colonial history, and bustling modern new towns.

The rides vary in length from 8 to 30 miles and are laid out for a leisurely half-day or so of bicycling with ample opportunities for resting at points of scenic or historical interest or at parks and beaches. For new riders there is a special guide to traffic-free paths that will simplify getting acquainted with bicycling. Each ride description includes a map, detailed road instructions, and information on its length, duration, terrain, and traffic conditions. These are accompanied by a general description of the ride area, its points of interest, and, where necessary, the difficulties that can be expected along the way.

An Overview

Ralph Henry Gabriel, in his excellent little book, *The Evolution of Long Island*, suggests that the character of the island stems from the interplay of the physical force of the surrounding sea and the social force of people and ideas issuing from New York City. The rides in this book explore the most interesting results of this mingling to provide the cyclist with a mosaic of experiences of what Long Island is and was.

Geologically, the island is known for its long, wide, white sand beaches on the Atlantic, its craggy inlets and harbors on Long Island Sound, and the flat terrain between — the result of glacial actions eons ago. The remains of the activity are visible on several of the rides: at Wading River and other points along the Sound shore where the cliffs carved from glacial debris stand silently facing the Sound; at Lake Ronkonkoma, which resulted from the filling of a hole left by a glacial fragment; and in the convoluted peninsulas and harbors seen on the western north-shore rides. The outwash beaches of the south shore of the Atlantic, Long Island's premiere summer attraction, are toured in the Montauk and Hampton rides of the east end, further west at Smith Point, and at Long Beach near the New York City border. Soils formed from glacial deposits were later developed into rich farmlands such as those seen on the rides through Wading River, Riverhead, Mattituck, Southold, and Orient on the island's north fork, and Bridgehampton on the south fork.

Farming and fishing supported the island's early settlers, and a good deal remains of the colonial past on the ride routes through the island's eastern parts at Southold and Southampton and north shore at Stony Brook, Port Jefferson, Smithtown, Huntington, and Northport. Other ride routes go through areas whose attractions date from more recent times, tracing the advance of urban development from New York City eastward on former farmland and scrub. Thus we get the estates seen on the rides through Great Neck, Manhasset, Glen Cove, and Oyster Bay on the north shore, neatly designed Garden City on the Hempstead Plains of Nassau County, and on the south shore, the closely packed communities of the Five Towns and Long Beach and the suburban sprawl along Merrick Road from Freeport to Seaford. The still-continuing expansion is evident further east in the rides through the Lake Ronkonkoma area, Great River, and Smith Point.

The evolution of Long Island continues, of course, but the underlying causes of change remain. No doubt these ride routes in the future will traverse communities vastly different from those that exist today—but they will probably be just as interesting for the cyclist to explore.

About the Directions

To the greatest extent possible, the ride material is presented to ease map and road direction reading when underway. Accordingly, the maps are located directly opposite the ride directions, and in most cases the directions are presented on a single page. Further, the directions are segmented to allow point-to-point riding. In almost all cases, these points on the road are clearly visible road signs, although in a few places unique landmarks or other features are used. It is suggested that the description of the ride be read in its entirety before riding to know beforehand the points of interest along the way (also noted on the maps), doing away with the need to refer to this material while pedaling.

The mileages in the ride directions are approximate distances. In most of the rides alternate, shorter routes are also provided. The time indicated is approximate pedaling time while cycling at a sight-seeing pace. It does not include extended rests or time at points of interest. Hilly terrain implies a ride in which the casual weekend cyclist will encounter some hills that will probably have to be walked; moderately hilly has less strenuous hills; rides designated as flat should be no problem at all. All the rides have been laid out to minimize riding in traffic, but even so, most rides have one or more segments in which some traffic will be encountered. The directions give a realistic assessment of what can be expected.

A Note on Safety

Traffic is heaviest in Nassau and western Suffolk but must be anticipated in all areas. The requirements for safe riding are simple enough—a bicycle in good working condition, defensive and alert riding, and a measure of common sense. The roads are there for autos and bicycles alike, and the cyclist is responsible no less than the motorist for full knowledge of, and conformance with, the rules of the road. Cyclists should:

- Ride on the right in the direction of traffic.
- Use hand signals when turning.
- Obey traffic signals and stop signs.
- When riding in a group, keep to the right in single file, keeping an adequate distance between riders.
- Make sure your bicycle has reliable brakes, a bell or horn for warning, and a headlight and rear and side reflectors for night riding.
- Wear a protective helmet and bright clothing.

In addition, everyone should be prepared for common bicycling hazards such as sandy patches on curves, potholes and sewer gratings, railroad-track crossings, and in urban areas, the sudden opening of parked car doors. Keep in mind that traffic is lightest on Sunday mornings, making the rides most enjoyable during these hours.

Although the roads should be shared equally, the realities of bicycling suggest that the rider not argue too strongly with motorized traffic for the right-of-way — it makes sense to yield. Finally, if you are at all unsure of your capability at bicycling, it is advisable to practice on the described traffic-free paths before attempting street riding.

*   *   *

While these thirty rides by no means exhaust the interesting bicycling routes that could be explored on Long Island, they would probably rank high on most cyclists' lists of the best the island has to offer.

1. Great Neck

Number of miles: 13
Approximate pedaling time: 2 hours
Terrain: Moderately hilly
Surface: Good
Traffic: Heavy in town, moderate elsewhere
Things to see: Saddle Rock Grist Mill, Stepping Stone Park,
U.S. Merchant Marine Academy

This is a pleasant ride around the Great Neck Peninsula, an area very much in demand by people who wish to remain within easy traveling distance of New York City while living in gracious suburban surroundings. There are outstanding water views all along its coasts on Little Neck Bay, Mahassett Bay, and Long Island Sound. From its northwest shore one can even see New York's skyscrapers and bridges. There are not many areas that can match Great Neck in convenience and charm, a fact that is reflected in the price of real estate and housing hereabouts.

The ride begins in the Shoreward parking lot south of the railroad station in the village of Great Neck Plaza. Parking is avai-lable to all on Sundays but is limited to Great Neck residents on weekdays and Saturdays. There are other parking lots, however, in shopping centers along Great Neck Road west of Middle Neck Road. Great Neck Plaza is the shopping and commuting center of the peninsula, and so it can be quite crowded and heavily trafficked. Once out of this immediate area, however, things quiet down.

From Great Neck Plaza the ride goes north on Bayview Avenue to the Saddle Rock Grist Mill. This is one of the most popular historical attractions on Long Island because it maintains the feel of handmade colonial buildings and the workaday world of the past. Corn is ground at the mill for demonstration purposes, and the various processes of milling, historic and current, are described in attractive displays.

How to get there: Exit 25 on Northern State Parkway, north on Lakeville Road, across Northern Boulevard (Route 25A) onto Middle Neck Road to South Station Plaza. Right two blocks to starting point at Shoreward parking field.

DIRECTIONS FOR THE RIDE:

- Start at the Shoreward parking field two blocks east of Middle Neck Road, south of the railroad tracks on Shoreward Drive.
- Out of the Shoreward parking lot, right on Shoreward Drive, across Middle Neck Road onto Great Neck Road, to Cutter Mill Road.
- Right at Cutter Mill Road, which immediately merges with Bayview Avenue on the left, for about 1 3/4 miles on Bayview, to Grist Mill Lane on the left. Signs indicate the approach to the grist mill.
- Left on Grist Mill Lane to the Saddle Rock Grist Mill.
- Return to Bayview Avenue (which becomes West Shore Road further on), and go left over Saddle Rock Bridge for 1 1/4 miles to Kings Point Road.
- Right on Kings Point Road to Steamboat Road.
- Left on Steamboat Road to the Merchant Marine Academy.
- From the academy go left on Stepping Stone Lane, adjacent to Stepping Stone Park on the left, around to Kings Point Road.
- Left on Kings Point Road for about 1 1/2 miles to its end.
- Return on Kings Point Road for about 3/4 mile to Split Rock Drive on the left.
- Left on Split Rock Drive to Wildwood Road.
- Left on Wildwood Road, across Middle Neck Road, onto East Shore Road.
- Continue on East Shore Road for 3 1/4 miles along Manhasset Bay to Grace Avenue. About halfway along this leg, East Shore Road turns left at the junction with Hicks Lane.
- Right on Grace Avenue past the Colonial Road merge for about 1 mile to Barstow Road.
- Left on Barstow Road across North Station Plaza to Shoreward Drive on the left.
- Left on Shoreward Drive to the Shoreward parking lot and the ride starting point.

The ride proceeds north from the grist mill over the Saddle Rock Bridge to Stemboat Road and the U.S. Merchant Marine Academy. Its sixty-eight acres and several buildings are worth seeing, especially the former Walter Chrysler estate on Long Island Sound, now part of the academy grounds. In the spring and fall, regimental reviews can be viewed on Saturday mornings.

Immediately north of the academy is Stepping Stone Park. There is no better view of Long Island Sound from Great Neck than from this park. On summer Sundays, the Sound is alive with sailboats. The park abounds with frisbee players, toddlers, and New York Times readers, producing so pleasant a stop that many cyclists won't bother to go any further.

Those that do, however, can continue north on Kings Point Road to Kings Point. The road dead-ends at a very peaceful and tranquil community of attractive homes on an inlet of Long Island Sound. Proceeding south from here the ride continues through wooded Kings Point to the east shore of the peninsula on Manhasset Bay. On East Shore Road for half its length is a wetlands strip containing a variety of marsh vegetation and wildlife.

On reentering the village of Great Neck, the surroundings become more commercial. Grace Avenue, the last leg of the ride, is a challenging uphill climb that may have to be walked. There are plenty of places near Shoreward parking field, however, to get cool refreshments, and you might also enjoy a stroll through the hubbub of Great Neck's shopping area along Middle Neck Road.

2. Manhasset — Port Washington

Number of miles: 17 (short ride 11)
Approximate pedaling time: 3 1/2 hours (short ride 2 hours)
Terrain: Moderately hilly
Surface: Good
Traffic: Heavy in towns, moderate elsewhere
Things to see: North Hempstead Town Dock, Sands Point
      Preserve, Hempstead Harbor Park

This ride takes you through some of the finest residential areas on Long Island. The Port Washington peninsula, or Manhasset Neck, is the site of a number of communities of impressive homes and estates, some dating to the nineteenth century. This peninsula, with Great Neck to the west and Oyster Bay to the east, makes up the "Gold Coast" of Long Island, signifying a sumptuous lifestyle made famous by F. Scott Fitzgerald. A good deal of "Great Gatsby" ambience remains, especially in the Sands Point area at the northern end of the peninsula.

    The ride starts at Manhasset Green Park in the village of Manhasset and proceeds north on Plandome Road past Leeds Pond Preserve and the North Shore Science Museum in Plandome Manor. Plandome Road is narrow and shoulderless in this area and should be cycled with care. The causeway leading to the entrance of the preserve affords the first unobstructed view of Manhasset Bay. The preserve and museum offer guided walks through typical local wildlife habitats. Bicycling within the preserve is not allowed, however.

    Continuing north we arrive at the North Hempstead Town Dock at Port Washington. There are several excellent restaurants here, although the meals they offer are more suitable for dinner than for cyclists' light lunches. The dock itself runs out into Manhasset Bay and is a nice place to stop for a cold drink and view of the bay and private boats running in and out.

    We continue on Main Street from the town dock up a steep hill to Shore Road, which intersects from the left. Those wishing to

How to get there: Exit 27 on Northern State Parkway, north on Shelter Rock Road to Northern Boulevard, Route 25A. West on Northern Boulevard about 1/4 mile to Plandome Road on the right. North on Plandome Road approximately 1/4 mile to the Manhasset Green Park parking lot on the left.

DIRECTIONS FOR THE RIDE:

- Start from Manhasset Green Park on Plandome Road and Manhasset Avenue, just south of the Manhasset railroad station.
- Out to Plandome Road and left approximately 1 1/2 miles to Leeds Pond Preserve.
- From the preserve, continue right for about 1 1/4 miles on Plandome Road past the town dock to Shore Road on the left, at the beginning of the uphill section of Main Street in Port Washington.
- For the short ride, continue on Main Street for about 1 mile to Port Washington Boulevard. Go left on Port Washington Boulevard one block to Beacon Hill Road on the right. Go right on Beacon Hill Road to West Shore Road.
- For the full ride, continue left on Shore Road (which becomes Sands Point Road) for about 2 3/4 miles to Middle Neck Road.
- Go left on Middle Neck Road to its end, with Lighthouse Road on the left.
- Go left on Lighthouse Road around back to Middle Neck Road.
- Right on Middle Neck Road approximately 1 1/2 miles to Sands Point Preserve (Falaise) on the left, then 2 1/2 miles to Beacon Hill Road on the left in Port Washington.
- Go left on Beacon Hill Road 1 mile to West Shore Road.
- Continue on West Shore Road, bordering Hempstead Harbor, to Hempstead Harbor Park and Bar Beach, then on for about 3 miles to Old Northern Boulevard on the right, indicated by a "Truck Route" sign immediately past the Northern Boulevard overpass and Mott Avenue.
- Go right on Old Northern Boulevard to the merge with Northern Boulevard, Route 25A, then continue west on 25A about 1/4 mile to Port Washington Boulevard – Route 101.
- Go right on Port Washington Boulevard one block to Park Avenue in Munsey Park on the left.
- Go left on Park Avenue for about 2 miles to Plandome Road in Manhasset. Friends Meeting House and Onderdonk Mansion are on Northern Boulevard five blocks south of Park Avenue at Onderdonk Avenue.
- Go left on Plandome Road back to the ride starting point at Manhasset Green Park.

take the short ride should continue straight ahead on Main Street through Port Washington to Port Washington Boulevard, picking up the route again at Beacon Hill Road. The full ride continues north to Sands Point. An immediate change is evident on entering Sands Point, as the surroundings become almost rural. In this area is a mix of fine old homes and large new ones located on spacious and attractive grounds. At the end of Middle Neck Road we come to the very end of the peninsula at Sands Point. Lighthouse Road provides a striking water view and setting for the modernistic homes along it.

Proceeding south from Sands Point we come to the Sands Point Preserve, the site of Falaise, a large estate featuring a palatial French Normandy-style manor house built in 1923 for Henry F. Guggenheim. Reservations must be made in advance to see the mansion, but it is worth it if you are interested in examining the living conditions of the very wealthy—twenty-six rooms, Spanish and French furnishings, sculpture, paintings, sailing trophies, etc.

South from Falaise we come to Beacon Hill Road in Port Washington. This is a steep climb to the east side of the peninsula and may require some walking. From the top of the hill, West Shore Road sweeps down and around the edge of Hempstead Bay, offering a panoramic view along the way. Hempstead Harbor Park and Bar Beach are pleasant stops for resting after the Beacon Hill climb. To the right of West Shore Road, south of Bar Beach, is a grim example of what years of sand mining can do to such a scenic area. Notice the houses perched just back from the rim of the pit.

The last part of the ride goes along West Shore Road to the base of the peninsula and then heads west, back to Manhasset. Expect heavy traffic on the short segment on Northern Boulevard and Port Washington Boulevard into Munsey Park. Munsey Park, near Onderdonk Avenue and Northern Boulevard, is a pleasant, well-tended suburban community with lots of clipped grass and new homes. Toward the end of the Park Avenue leg is the Friends Meeting House, and next to it, the Onderdonk Mansion. The former, built in 1812, has the expected spare lean look and is in marked contrast to the columned robustness of the latter, built for Henry Gates Onderdonk in 1836.

3. Roslyn — Old Westbury

Number of miles: 8
Approximate pedaling time: 1 1/2 hours
Terrain: Moderately hilly
Surface: Good
Traffic: Moderate to heavy
Things to see: Robeson-Williams Gristmill, Roslyn Clock Tower,
     Roslyn Historic District, Old Westbury Gardens, Roslyn
     Air National Guard Station

The town of Roslyn is nestled at the head of Hempstead Harbor, almost hidden from view from the autos whizzing by it on Route 25A on the elevated Roslyn Viaduct. It is a delightful place, however, to savor a vestige of Long Island's past. Within a half mile or so of the village is one of the most extensive communities of colonial and nineteenth-century homes and buildings that can be found on Long Island. For cyclists, it is an excellent starting point and terminus for an interesting ride through the estate country of Old Westbury and attractive modern suburban communities.

The ride starts from any of the parking lots on Old Northern Boulevard in Roslyn. The village dates from colonial times when the stream flowing into Hempstead Harbor was harnessed for milling. As happened on this and many other streams, the mill formed the nucleus of commercial activity for the surrounding agricultural lands leading to the development of the town.

On Old Northern Boulevard stands the Robeson-Williams Gristmill. The mill was built around 1700 and has since been restored. To the west, toward Main Street, is Washington Manor on Northern Boulevard. The building dates from 1758 and is now a restaurant. Guess who slept here in the summer of 1790? Across the way is the Roslyn Clock Tower, built in 1895, and further along on Main Street, Roslyn's Historic District. On Main Street between Old Northern Boulevard and East Broadway, stand about forty homes built between 1690 and 1865. Some are in excellent condition, and several are being restored.

The ride continues on Main Street onto Roslyn Road, passing under the Long Island Railroad on an uphill climb, usually with heavy traffic, past Roslyn High School, to Roslyn Heights. After passing the Long Island Expressway and Northern State Parkway,

How to get there: Exit 29 on Northern State Parkway, north on Roslyn Road 1-3/4 miles to Old Northern Boulevard, Roslyn.

DIRECTIONS FOR THE RIDE:

- Start at one of the parking lots on Old Northern Boulevard in Roslyn.
- West from the parking lot to Main Street.
- Left on Main Street, which becomes Roslyn Road, through the Roslyn Historic District.
- Continue on Roslyn Road for about 2 3/4 miles, passing under the Long Island Railroad tracks and Long Island Expressway, and then over Northern State Parkway, to I. U. Willets Road.
- Left on I. U. Willets Road for approximately 2 miles, over Northern State Parkway to its end at Old Westbury Road.
- Left on Old Westbury Road to Old Westbury Gardens on the right.
- From Old Westbury Gardens, continue right on Old Westbury Road for about 3/4 mile, over the Long Island Expressway to Store Hill Road, the expressway (westbound) service road.
- Left on Store Hill Road, past Wheatley Road, for about 1/2 mile to Red Ground Road.
- Right on Red Ground Road for about 1 1/4 miles to the intersection with Glen Cove Road and Harbor Hill Road. (Red Ground Road goes left at the junction with Hastings Road, halfway along this leg.)
- Straight across the intersection onto Harbor Hill Road; then on past the Roslyn Air National Guard Station for about 1 1/2 miles back to Roslyn Road.
- Right on Roslyn Road to Roslyn Park on the right.
- Continue through the park and Paper Mill Road back to ride starting point.

we enter Albertson. Here we find a typical higher-priced, but somewhat bland, modern suburban community on flat terrain.

After turning left at I. U. Willets Road, the ride progresses into Old Westbury at Glen Cove Road, and an immediate change in landscape is noticed. There are fewer homes, more and larger trees, and in some spots, full forest growth.

Turning left on Old Westbury Road we come immediately to the Old Westbury Gardens and Mansion. This is the former estate of the Phipps family, containing a huge eighteenth-century Georgian-style manor house built in 1906 and acres of manicured lawns shaded by tall, graceful trees. The estate also contains a formal Italian garden and an arboretum. It's a good place to stop and rest and experience for a while the good life of the very wealthy.

From Old Westbury Gardens we continue on Old Westbury Road over the Long Island Expressway onto the expressway's westbound service road. This is a bleak, open stretch that is best crossed quickly to regain good cycling country at Red Ground Road. Along Red Ground Road are fine large homes and heavily treed estates. At its end is a wide intersection at which Red Ground, Glen Cove, and Harbor Hill roads meet. Go directly across onto Harbor Hill Road.

Along Harbor Hill Road are pleasant homes situated on rather hilly terrain. Suddenly, on the right, is the Roslyn Air National Guard Station, a military installation that seems completely out of place in such a peaceful and sheltered community. Harbor Hill Road continues down to Roslyn Road where we turn right, back toward Roslyn.

We enter the Roslyn Historic District at Main Street. Down a short way is Paper Mill Road and Roslyn Park on the right. On Paper Mill Road is Valentine House, built around 1800 and rebuilt around 1865. It now houses the Roslyn Village Hall. Further on in Roslyn Park is a replica of the Onderdonk Paper Mill, New York's first paper mill, built around 1770. From here we continue back to Northern Boulevard and the starting point of the ride. You might be ready by this time for a good meal in one of the fine restaurants in the area.

4. Glen Cove — Sea Cliff

Number of miles: 21 (short ride 13)
Approximate pedaling time: 3 hours (short ride 2 hours)
Terrain: Hilly
Surface: Good
Traffic: Heavy in towns, moderate elsewhere
Things to see: Garvies Point Museum and Preserve, East Island,
    St. John's Episcopal Church, Memorial Park (Sea Cliff)

Glen Cove dates from earliest colonial times, its first settlers appearing in the late 1600s. Because of its water access it grew as a thriving port and commercial center into one of the major towns of Long Island. Sea Cliff dates from the mid-1800s when the heights south of Glen Cove, overlooking Hempstead Harbor, were used by a Methodist group as a summer meeting ground. The attractions of the area induced some of the group to build permanent residences, which in turn became the center of a popular summer resort community attracting visitors from New York and elsewhere every year.

Glen Cove and Sea Cliff have, of course, changed dramatically since those days, Glen Cove especially having long since developed a busy urban environment. But traces of the past remain, the surrounding areas are still attractive, and the water view is as expansive as it has always been.

The ride begins at the Garvies Point Museum and Preserve in Glen Cove and proceeds north. Be ready for some hill climbing almost immediately. We enter estate country at New Woods Road and Dosoris Lane; on the right is a former Pratt Mansion (there were several Pratt family mansions in the area) now used as the Harrison House Conference Center. At the end of Dosoris Lane, if we go left, we traverse two small causeways and come to East Island, the site of a former home of J. P. Morgan. It is said that more than one hundred employees were required to tend the large mansion that once stood here and the supporting dairy and agricultural activities that Morgan instituted on the island. There are beautiful water views on all the drives that ring the island.

Returning to Lattingtown Road we come to the Glen Cove Golf Course and Recreation Area and then pass estate grounds for a mile or so. This portion of the ride is exceptionally pleasant in

How to get there: Exit 39 on the Long Island Expressway approximately 7 miles north on Guinea Woods Road and Glen Cove Road to the city of Glen Cove. Follow signs to Garvies Point Museum and Preserve.

DIRECTIONS FOR THE RIDE:

- Start from Garvies Point Museum and Preserve. Go out of the parking lot onto Barry Drive four blocks to McLoughlin Street.
- Right on McLoughlin Street half a block to Germaine Street.
- Left on Germaine Street one block to Landing Road.
- Right on Landing Road for about 3/4 mile to Crescent Beach Road.
- Left on Crescent Beach Road for about 1 mile to New Woods Road on the right.
- Right on New Woods Road for about 3/4 mile to Dosoris Lane.
- Left on Dosoris Lane for approximately 3/4 mile to its end at the Lattingtown Road intersection.
- Left at the intersection for a 2 3/4 mile circuit of East Island.
- Return to the Lattingtown Road-Dosoris Lane Intersection and continue on Lattingtown Road for 2 1/2 miles past St. John's Episcopal Church, to Ludlam Lane on the left.
- Left on Ludlam Lane to the merge with Birch Hill Road.
- Continue right on Birch Hill Road (which becomes Piping Rock Road) for 1 1/4 miles to Friends Meeting House at Duck Pond Road, then on for 2 miles to Chicken Valley Road. (Those taking the short ride go right on Duck Pond Road, over the railroad tracks, onto Town Path to Glen Street, right on Glen Street to School Street, then follow Garvies Point Museum signs back to the starting point.)
- Right on Chicken Valley Road past the Brookville Country Club 3/4 miles to Cedar Swamp Road (Route 107).
- Right on Cedar Swamp Road to Glen Head Road on the left.
- Left on Glen Head Road, which becomes Glenwood Road just past the railroad tracks, down the long hill to Shore Avenue.
- Right at the Long Island Lighting Company plant on Shore Avenue, which becomes Prospect Avenue, for about 1 3/4 miles to Sea Cliff Avenue.
- Right on Sea Cliff Avenue for 1 mile to Glen Cove Avenue.
- Left on Glen Cove Avenue for about 3/4 mile to Charles Street. (From here signs indicate the way back.)
- Left on Charles Street to The Place, to Elwood, to Landing Road.
- Left on Landing Road to Germaine Street, McLoughlin Street, and Barry Drive back to the ride starting point.

midsummer when the road is shaded a cool green by the large over-hanging trees. At the intersection of Lattingtown and Overlook roads is St. John's Episcopal Church of Lattingtown on the right, a beautiful stone structure comfortably settled into the hillside. Further south we enter Locust Valley, containing some interesting antique stores and bookshops, where lunch can be obtained. Just south of here is a Friends Meeting House, built in 1877, looming up on the right at Piping Rock and Duck Pond roads.

Those taking the short ride right at this point toward Glen Cove via Duck Pond Road, Town Park, glen street, and School Street, and from there follow the markers back to Garvies Point Museum and Preserve. The main ride continues south along Piping Rock Road to Chicken Valley Road, passing the Brookville Country Club and attractive homes on beautifully treed acres. Cycle these roads with care since they are shoulderless and at times have heavy traffic.

At Glen Head Road the neighborhood change abruptly to more conventional housing with the usual mix of stores and small businesses common to most of suburban Long island. Glen Head Road is an uphill climb to a long downhill run to Glenwood Landing and Hempstead Harbor.

We go right at the giant Long Island Lighting Company generating plant, so out of place here, along Shore Road to Sea Cliff. Along the way is Tappan Beach where we get a good view across Hempstead Harbor of the Port Washington sand pits. At Sea Cliff we start an uphill climb on Prospect Avenue, continuing onto Sea Cliff Avenue. At the intersection of Sea Cliff and Prospect avenues is memorial Park, a small patch of grass with a spectacular view of Long Island Sound, with Westchester visible on the horizon and Port Washington to the left. It is best to walk the 1/2 mile through Sea Cliff to observe closely its carefully maintained ornate Carpenter Gothic Victorian homes.

At Glen Cove Avenue we turn left and return to Glen Cove and Garvies Point Museum and Preserve. The half mile downhill on Glen Cove Avenue should be cycled with care since there is usually heavy and fast traffic. At the museum and preserve you might be interested in viewing the exhibits of regional geology and Indian archaeology, and if energy remains, in strolling the seventy-two acres of varied terrain and vegetation typical of Long Island.

5. Mill Neck — Center Island

Number of miles: 20 (short ride 10)
Approximate pedaling time: 3 1/2 hours (short ride 2 hours)
Terrain: Hilly
Surface: Good; sandy in places
Traffic: Moderate to heavy
Things to see: Planting Fields Arboretum, Bailey Arboretum, Ransom Beach, Center Island, Seawanhaka Corinthian Yacht Club

The north shore of western Long Island is lined with enclosed bays, promontories, necks, and peninsulas on which many picturesque communities have developed. This ride explores some of the most interesting of these along an inland and water's-edge route through the villages of Mill Neck, Bayville, and Center Island. It traverses beautifully wooded areas and several beaches on Long Island Sound and Oyster Bay. The way is sometimes hilly, but the views are worth the effort.

The ride begins at the municipal parking lot in the village of Oyster Bay, on South Street, just north of East Main (Audrey) Street. We proceed out of the lot through the village, following signs to the Planting Fields Arboretum. Planting Fields, formerly the estate of W.R. Coe, features magnificent trees, a large collection of vines and shrubs, including an assemblage of rhodo-dendrons and azaleas, and several tropical-plant greenhouses.

From the arboretum we continue along Planting Fields Road west through Mill Neck. Mill Neck, like neighboring Matinecock and Locust Valley, is a heavily treed and hilly area and the site of many large and attractive homes. After an uphill climb on Oyster Bay Road, we go onto Bayville Road and come to Bailey Arboretum. For those who didn't get enough at Planting Fields, Bailey features a nineteenth-century house and a collection of rare plants.

From Bailey Arboretum we continue north on Bayville Road for a long downhill run into Bayville. (Those wishing to take a shorter ride can return to Oyster Bay through a hilly, but extremely pleasant, wooded area on Factory Pond Road and Feeks Lane [Cleft Road]. This also eliminates most of the heavily trafficked and narrow West Shore segment of the full ride). The environment changes abruptly

How to get there: Exit 36 on Northern State Parkway, or Exit 43 on the Long Island Expressway, north on Oyster Bay Road about 2 1/2 miles to the village of Syosset. Go through Syosset on Berry Hill Road for about 4 miles to South Street in Oyster Bay. Go right on South Street past East Main Street (Audrey Avenue) to the municipal parking lot indicated on the right.

DIRECTIONS FOR THE RIDE:

- Start from the municipal parking lot on South Street in Oyster Bay. Left on South Street to West Main Street.
- Right on West Main Street to Lexington on the left.
- Left on Lexington to Mill River Road and sign indicating the way to the Planting Fields Arboretum.
- Right on Mill River Road about 1/2 mile to Glen Cove Road.
- Right on Glen Cove Road 1/2 mile to Planting Fields Road.
- Left on Planting Fields Road to the arboretum.
- Left (west) from the arboretum on Planting Fields Road to Chicken Valley Road.
- Right on Chicken Valley Road onto Oyster Bay Road, following sign to Locust Valley and the Bailey Arboretum.
- Continue on Oyster Bay Road over Francis Pond for about 1 3/4 miles to Bayville Road, just past the overpass.
- Right on Bayville Road, following signs to the arboretum.
- Right from the arboretum on Bayville Road 1 3/4 miles to Bayville Avenue. A bike path exists for this segment north of Horse Hollow Road. (Those taking the short ride, turn right from Bayville Road onto Factory Pond Road about 3/4 mile north of the arboretum. Continue on Factory Pond for about 1 mile to Feeks Lane [Cleft Road]. Left on Feeks Lane for 1 3/4 miles to West Shore Road. Right on West Shore onto West Main then South Street in Oyster Bay.)
- Proceed on Bayville Avenue past Ransom Beach, Ludlam Avenue, and Center Island Beach to the entrance to Center Island.
- Continue on Center Island Road for 2 1/2 miles to the turnaround, then return. Seawanhaka Road and the Seawanhaka Corinthian Yacht Club are about halfway along.
- Go back on Bayville Avenue to West Harbor Drive, just past the Center Island Beach parking lot.
- Left on West Harbor Drive 1 mile to Ludlam Avenue.
- Left on Ludlam Avenue over bridge onto West Shore Road.
- Continue on West Shore Road for about 3 miles, under railroad overpass and past Mill Pond, onto West Main Street.
- Continue on West Main Street to South Street.
- Left on South Street to the municipal parking lot.

at Bayville from wooded hills to sandy seashore.

On the left is Ransom Beach on Long Island Sound. Opposite the beach is a string of restaurants and snack bars usually busy with beach patrons and cyclists.

Further along on Bayville Avenue we proceed through a busier, crowded section. At one time this was primarily a summer vacation colony. It is fast becoming a year-round community, but most of the housing reflects its earlier use. We continue on Bayville Avenue past the Renaissance, a large health spa, straight through the Ludlam Avenue intersection and its perpetual traffic jam, and continue east. Traffic gets lighter past Ludlam Avenue as the neighborhood becomes less densely populated. After a mile or so we come to the Center Island Beach parking lot and boat launching ramps. The town beach straddles the peninsula and runs for 3/4 mile to the entrance to the village of Center Island.

As the turnaround and police station suggest, motorists are urged to turn at this point and head back to Bayville. Most cyclists, however, continue on Center Island Road, which runs for about 2 1/2 miles into the peninsula. It is a beautiful shaded stretch, flanked by large homes and estates. About a mile along, on the left, is Seawanhaka Road, which runs past the Seawanhaka Corinthian Yacht Club, one of the oldest and most prestigious yacht clubs in the United States, to Cold Spring Harbor. From here, on the right in the distance, is Cove Neck, the site of Theodore Roosevelt's estate, Sagamore Hill.

From Center Island we head back to Oyster Bay. We swing around Bayville on West Harbor Road, heading for West Shore Road in Mill Neck. At the bridge leading to West Shore Road we get a beautiful view of Mill Neck Bay on the right and Oyster Bay Harbor on the left. The harbor view continues for the length of the ride on West Shore Road into Oyster Bay. Ride with care on this road since it is narrow, shoulderless, and often has heavy traffic.

6. Oyster Bay — Brookville

Number of miles: 18 (short ride 13)
Approximate pedaling time: 4 hours (short ride 2 1/2 hours)
Terrain: Hilly
Surface: Good; some sandy sections
Traffic: Light to moderate
Things to see: Nature Conservancy Preserve, Sagamore Hill, Theodore Roosevelt Memorial Sanctuary, Trailside Museum, Oyster Bay, Planting Fields Arboretum

It has been more than sixty years since Theodore Roosevelt lived at Sagamore Hill. Since that time the estate has been declared a National Historic Site and has become one of the major attractions of Long Island. It is the high point of this exceptionally scenic ride through the village of Oyster Bay and the adjoining villages of Brookville and Muttontown.

The village of Oyster Bay dates from colonial times and retains a decidedly early northshore flavor: a mix of New England colonial architecture, a salt-air environment, and hilly and heavily wooded terrain. Brookville and Muttontown, to the west and south of Oyster Bay, are large wooded tracts dotted with estates and fine old homes. The countryside is covered with stands of towering graceful trees, which during summer make every road a delightfully cool tunnel of mixed sunlight and shade. Because of the beauty of the area, and its challenging terrain, it is a favorite with cyclists.

The ride starts from the Syosset railroad-station parking lot, heading east onto Cold Spring Road to White Oak Tree Road in Laurel Hollow. White Oak Tree Road is a narrow, quiet lane with new homes set back almost out of sight in the surrounding foliage. Toward its end we go through a Nature Conservancy Preserve in which it is possible to experience, for however short a time, the quiet and solitude of untouched Long Island woodland.

We pass over Route 25A and proceed onto Cove Road, a smooth gentle downhill run through the beginning of an area of large homes and estates. Turning right at the sign for Sagamore Hill, at Cove Neck Road, we obtain our first view of Oyster Bay Harbor, a wide expanse of blue water flecked with small sailboats and powerboats. Cycle with care here since Cove Neck Road is narrow and shoulderless. Beyond it is the village of Oyster Bay. We turn right at the sign for Sagamore Hill and come to a steep hill indeed. Be prepared to walk up this stretch.

How to get there: Exit 36 on Northern State parkway, or Exit 43 on the Long Island Expressway, north on Oyster Bay Road (which becomes Jackson Avenue north of Route 25) about 2 1/2 miles to the village of Syosset. Proceed over the railroad tracks and then right into the station parking lot.

DIRECTIONS FOR THE RIDE:

- Start from the Syosset railroad-station parking lot. Proceed to Cold Spring Road at the end of the lot near the firehouse.
- Right on Cold Spring Road, following the sign to Cold Spring Harbor, for about 2 miles to White Oak Tree Road.
- Left on White Oak Tree Road for about 1 1/4 miles to Route 25A and Cove Road, and then on for about 2 miles to a sign indicating Sagamore Hill.
- Right at the sign onto Cove Neck Road for approximately 1 3/4 miles to Sagamore Hill, then return to the Roosevelt grave and Memorial Sanctuary.
- Left (west) from the grave site on Cove Road (later East Main Street) toward the village of Oyster Bay.
- Continue on East Main Street past Oyster Bay High School, Christ Episcopal Church, and First Presbyterian Church, to South Street.
- Left on South Street to West Main Street. (For the short ride, proceed about 1/2 mile up South Street to Berry Hill Road. Go left on Berry Hill for about 4 miles to Eastwoods-Muttontown Road and left to the station parking lot.)
- Right on West Main Street past Raynham Hall to Lexington.
- Left on Lexington to Mill River Road and a sign indicating the way to the Planting Fields Arboretum.
- Right on Mill River Road about 1/2 mile to Glen Cove Road.
- Right on Glen Cove Road to Planting Fields Road.
- Left on Planting Fields Road to the gate of the arboretum.
- Left (west) from the arboretum on Planting Fields Road to Chicken Valley Road.
- Left on Chicken Valley Road to Wolver Hollow Road.
- Left on Wolver Hollow Road for about 1 3/4 miles through upper Brookville, across Route 25A onto Brookville Road, bearing left at the fork with Wheatley Road.
- Continue on Brookville Road for about 1 1/4 miles to Muttontown Road, opposite the Jane B. Francke bird sanctuary.
- Left on Muttontown Road through Muttontown for about 1 1/2 miles to Route 106, Jericho-Oyster Bay Road.
- Continue across Route 106 onto Eastwoods-Muttontown Road for about 1 1/2 miles across Split Rock Road in Syosset, onto Cold Spring Road to the railroad parking lot.

Sagamore Hill is always a pleasure to visit. The house, built in 1885, exudes an aura of Victorian warmth and comfort, the simply landscaped grounds are spacious and well tended, and there is a grand view of the harbor and Long Island Sound. The site also features the Old Orchard Museum, built in 1938, the former home of Roosevelt's son, Theodore Roosevelt, Jr.

From Sagamore Hill, we return to Cove Road and the Roosevelt grave site, and next to it, the Theodore Roosevelt Memorial Sanctuary and Trailside Museum, owned by the National Audubon Society. The grave site is simple and quiet, the sanctuary offers 12 acres of undisturbed land containing a variety of trees and bird species, and the museum displays numerous Long Island plants and animals. The trails are open to society members only.

From here we proceed to the village of Oyster Bay. The road is lined with new and old homes of Victorian and other nineteenth-century styles, with an estate here and there. On East Main Street we pass Oyster Bay High School, a huge brick structure, Christ Episcopal Church on the right, and the First Presbyterian Church on the left. The former church, a slate-roofed stone struture, dates from 1879 and was attended by Roosevelt for many years; the latter is an interesting example of Carpenter Gothic on a large scale. On West Main Street is Raynham Hall, a gray saltbox home dating from 1738, where British forces maintained quarters during the Revolutionary War. All along East and West Main streets are interesting Victorian and even older homes.

From Oyster Bay, those taking the short ride proceed south on South Street to Berry Hill Road, following this all the way back to Syosset. The full ride continues on to Planting Fields Arboretum. Planting Fields, the former estate of W. R. Coe, features hundreds of acres of trees and shrubs on wide lawns, an extensive collection of rhododendrons and azaleas, and a number of greenhouses with collections of tropical plants.

The remainder of the ride goes through Upper Brookville and Muttontown, along 7 miles of rather narrow and shoulderless but always scenic roads back to Syosset. Country clubs, estates, and large homes abound on all sides. Just past the Woodcrest Club we reenter Syosset, the ride starting point.

7. Huntington — Lloyd Neck

Number of miles: 19 (8 1/2 without Lloyd Neck)
Approximate pedaling time: 4 hours (2 hours without Lloyd Neck)
Terrain: Hilly
Surface: Good; some sandy sections
Traffic: Heavy in Huntington and Cold Spring Harbor, moderate
     elsewhere
Things to see: Huntington Harbor, Eagle Hill School (Coindre
     Hall), Henry Lloyd Manor House, Black Oak Tree, Target
     Rock National Wildlife Refuge, Cold Spring Harbor
     Whaling Museum

Huntington and Lloyd Neck make up one of the several peninsulas that jut into Long Island Sound from Long Island's north shore. It is a charming and picturesque area that is rich in colonial history and architecture and that offers superb water views.

The ride heads north from Huntington Village toward Huntington Harbor. From West Shore Road we get a continuous view of the harbor and in the early morning hours the hundreds of small sailboats and pleasure craft moored chock-a-block on its surface. In good sailing weather it's interesting to watch the feats of seamanship performed by these squadrons as they maneuver to reach Long Island Sound simultaneously.

At Browns Road we start a 1/2 mile uphill climb that can be relieved somewhat by a stop at the Eagle Hill School. It is housed in a large French-Normandy — style building known as Coindre Hall, built around 1915 as a residence for George McKesson Brown, a New York drug manufacturer. From the '30s through the '60s it was used by a Catholic order as a school for boys, and in 1970 it was acquired by Suffolk County. It then became the Harbor Arts Center, which the county operated as an art school and archaeological and Indian museum until 1981, when it was obtained by its present owners. Looking east from the rear of the building, past the old estate boat house at the water's edge, we have a stunning view of Huntington Harbor and its outlet to Long Island Sound at Sandy Point.

From Browns Road we continue north along Neck Road on the traffic-free Lloyd Harbor bike path, through an attractive

How to get there: North on Route 110 from Exit 40 on Northern State Parkway, or Exit 49 on the Long Island Expressway, about 6 1/2 miles to Elm Street, one block south of Main Street, Route 25A, in the village of Huntington. A municipal parking lot, indicated by a sign on Route 110, is half a block up on Elm Street.

DIRECTIONS FOR THE RIDE:

- The ride starts at the municipal parking lot on Elm Street, one block south of Main Street (Route 25A) in Huntington.
- Proceed out of the parking lot onto Elm Street and then right to New York Avenue, then right again to Main Street.
- Right on Main Street about 1/2 mile to Sabbath Day Path on the left, just past the Old First Presbyterian Church.
- Left on Sabbath Day Path to merge with Park Avenue on the right. Continue left on Park about 1/2 mile to merge with New York Avenue and the intersection with Mill Dam Road at Nathan Hale Rock.
- Left on Mill Dam Road at the head of Huntington Harbor about 1/2 mile to West Shore Road.
- Right on West Shore Road about 1 mile onto Browns Road.
- Continue on Browns Road to Eagle Hill School (Coindre Hall) opposite Bayberry Lane, then on to Southdown Road.
- Jog left on Southdown Road to John Dave's Lane on the right.
- Right on John Dave's Lane to West Neck Road.
- Right on West Neck Road, following bike-route signs for about 3 1/4 miles to Lloyd Neck and Lloyd Harbor Road. The Seminary of the Immaculate Conception is on the right.
- Continue on Lloyd Harbor Road (no bike path), passing Caumsett State Park and Lloyd Manor House, for about 2 1/2 miles to its end, at the Black Oak Tree and Target Rock National Wildlife Refuge.
- Return on Lloyd Harbor Road and West Neck Road to Middle Hollow Road on the right, opposite the police station.
- Right on Middle Hollow Road to its end at Jennings Road.
- Right on Jennings Road for about 1/4 mile, following the yellow traffic divider left onto Snake Hill Road, then on for about 3/4 mile downhill to its end at Shore Road.
- Left on Shore Road for about 3/4 mile to Main Street (Route 25A) in Cold Spring Harbor.
- Left on Main Street to the Whaling Museum, then on, following Route 25A signs, 1 1/2 miles back to New York Avenue (Route 110) in Huntington.
- Right on New York Avenue to the Elm Street municipal parking lot and starting point of the ride.

wooded area of fine new homes and several well-preserved Victorian- and colonial-style structures. Opposite Lloyd Harbor Village Park is the Seminary of the Immaculate Conception of the Roman Catholic Diocese of Brooklyn. The grounds are closed to the public, but from the entry road on West Neck Road you can get a good view of the impressive brick Italianate structure in a parklike setting that forms the nucleus of the seminary.

Just past West Neck Beach the path runs on a narrow isthmus to Lloyd Harbor Road on Lloyd Neck. The bike path ends at this point. Lloyd Harbor Road has some traffic and is hilly and narrow, but it's a scenic stretch going through lightly developed woods, with Lloyd Harbor sparkling through the foliage.

Along this road we find the Joseph Lloyd House, a stately white clapboard colonial structure dating from 1760, and just further on, the original Henry Lloyd Manor House, a more modest shingled saltbox structure dating from 1711. Just east of these is the entrance to Caumsett State Park, a former estate of Marshall Field. Its 1,500 acres offer miles of bike paths and terrific Long Island Sound views. At the very end of Lloyd Harbor Road is the famous Black Oak Tree, said to be the largest black oak in the United States (20 feet in circumference; 100 feet tall; 150-foot branch spread). Past the Black Oak Tree, up the road, is the Target Rock National Wildlife Refuge. The preserve contains formal gardens and trails through typical Long Island landforms and vegetation.

Retracing our way from Lloyd Neck on West Neck Road, we come to Middle Hollow Road and start a long uphill trek to Jennings Road. Then comes a long, steep, twisting descent on aptly named Snake Hill Road. Be sure to check your brakes before starting down this exhilarating stretch. At the bottom we come to Shore Road and the Cold Spring Harbor Beach Club.

Continuing south on Shore Road we turn left on heavily traveled Main Street (Route 25A) in Cold Spring Harbor and pass charming Victorian and colonial homes and shops that recapture the country village atmosphere that existed here a century ago. The buildings now house fine boutiques, craft shops, and restaurants. On the left on the way back to Huntington is the Cold Spring Harbor Whaling Museum, featuring a plethora of displays on whaling as it was once practiced. After one last hill climb on Main Street, we pass the Huntington Country Club and return to Huntington and the ride starting point.

After the ride it is interesting to see some of the many colonial structures maintained in the village. It is also worthwhile visiting the Heckscher Museum in Heckscher Park at Main and Park streets for its fine collection of paintings.

8. Northport — Eaton's Neck

Number of miles: 17 (6 1/2 without Eaton's Neck)
Approximate pedaling time: 3 1/2 hours (1 1/2 hours without Eaton's Neck)
Terrain: Hilly (with narrow roads on Eaton's Neck)
Surface: Good; some sandy sections
Traffic: Heavy in Northport, moderate elsewhere
Things to see: Bayview Avenue, beaches, Northport Harbor

Northport is a pleasant old village nestled some distance north of the main traffic arteries of the north shore. It is located at the base of Eaton's Neck peninsula, which juts out 3 miles into Long Island Sound. English and New England settlers first arrived here in the 1600s, and in time the village became a major boat-building and oystering center. Northport and Eaton's Neck peninsula offer a most interesting ride because of the combination of historical atmosphere, magnificent water views, and varied terrain found in few other places on Long Island.

The ride starts from the parking lot at the foot of Main Street on Northport Harbor. It proceeds north on charming Bayview Avenue, lined with nineteenth-century homes, to James Street. James Street is a difficult steep hill climb and is best walked. All along James Street and Ocean Avenue, which follows it, however, is a terrific view of Northport Bay and Eaton's Neck to the north. On clear days the Connecticut hills are visible on the horizon. Unfortunately there is also an unobstructed view of the Long Island Lighting Company's four-stack Northport electric generating plant, a mass of steel and concrete completely at odds with its surroundings.

Continuing north on Eaton's Neck Road we go down from the heights of Ocean Avenue to the Asharoken isthmus, which connects Northport to Eaton's Neck. As we enter the village of Asharoken we pass Steers Northport Village Beach, and adjoining it, Asharoken Beach. From here we continue on Asharoken Avenue on the narrow strip of beach that separates Long Island Sound from Northport Bay. At points the isthmus is no more than 150 feet wide, with an abrupt drop-off to the sound on the right and comfortable summer cottages and homes on the left. This is a difficult stretch for cyclists since the road is shoulderless and extremely narrow.

How to get there: Exit 42 on Northern State Parkway, north on East Deer Park Road to Jericho Turnpike (Route 25), then right 2 miles to Elwood Road. Left on Elwood Road for about 4 1/2 miles to Fort Salonga Road (Route 25A). Left on Fort Salonga Road about 1/2 mile to Woodbine Avenue. Right on Woodbine Avenue about 1/2 mile to Main Street, Northport. Park in public parking lot at the foot of Main Street.

DIRECTIONS FOR THE RIDE:

- Start from one of the public parking lots at the foot of Main Street on Northport Harbor.
- Go left from Main Street on Bayview Avenue about 1/2 mile to its end at James Street.
- Right on James Street 1/2 mile uphill to Ocean Avenue.
- Left on Ocean Avenue about 1/2 mile to Eaton's Neck Road.
- Left on Eaton's Neck Road about 1/2 mile downhill past Steers Northport Village Beach and then Asharoken Beach onto Asharoken Avenue.
- Continue about 3 miles on Asharoken Avenue on narrow isthmus to Eaton's Neck Road in village of Eaton's Neck.
- Continue on Eaton's Neck Road for about 1 mile, to Tudor Road on the right.
- Right on Tudor Road to its end at Birmingham Drive.
- Right on Birmingham Drive to Hobart Beach.
- Return to Northport via Birmingham, Tudor, Eaton's Neck Road, Asharoken Avenue, and Eaton's Neck Road, going past Ocean Avenue to Waterside Road on the left, past the LILCO plant entrance road.
- Left on Waterside about 1 mile, with Crab Meadow Park and Golf Course on the right, to Crab Meadow Beach.
- Return on Waterside, going left past Eaton's Neck Road, continuing on Waterside for about 1/2 mile to Norwood Avenue on the right.
- Right on Norwood Avenue for about 1 mile to Main Street.
- Right on Main Street, past the Northport Historical Society Museum, to its end at Northport Harbor and the ride starting point.

As we progress into Eaton's Neck the terrain abruptly changes from flat sandy shore to wooded hills. We continue on these ups and downs through Eaton's Neck, following the signs indicating the way to the town beach. After passing through a community of neat, modern homes we come to Hobart Beach at the end of the road. This is a good place to rest, and swim if you like, or just enjoy the views — Long Island Sound to the north, Lloyd Neck to the west, and a pleasant small boat-filled harbor to the south. Stretching out into Northport Harbor from Hobart Beach is a two-pronged peninsula known as "Sand City." There are no roads on it, and so it is an uncrowded swimming beach area where pleasure boaters often anchor.

Returning, we trace our way back through Eaton's Neck to the narrow strip of Asharoken Avenue and head back toward Northport, squarely facing the omnipresent stacks of the generating plant. We get an even closer view of these as we go past the plant on Eaton's Neck Road. Although the plant is an eyesore and a constant irritant to local residents, it provides a vital service, producing about one-third of the electric energy used on Long Island.

As we head north on Waterside Avenue, we pass the Crab Meadow Park and Golf Course with its manicured greens and stately trees, and then come to Crab Meadow Beach. It has a small snack bar in an attractive sand-colored cement and stucco beach house, complete with red-tiled roof, at which you can get hot dogs, hamburgers, and soft drinks.

From Crab Meadow Beach we head back on Waterside Avenue to Norwood Road and the center of Northport village. At the intersection of Main Street and Woodside Avenue is the Northport Historical Society Museum, featuring items of historical interest on Northport and its environs but also offering a detailed walking guide of the village. It is worthwhile to obtain this pamphlet and explore on foot the dozens of homes, commercial establishments, and stores dating from the early 1800s that line Main Street and Bayview and Woodbine avenues along Northport Harbor.

9. Smithtown — Nissequogue

Number of miles: 12
Approximate pedaling time: 3 hours
Terrain: Hilly
Surface: Good; some sandy sections
Traffic: Moderate to heavy
Things to see: "Bull" Smythe monument, St. James General Store, Old Nissequogue School, Village of the Branch

The town of Smithtown originally existed as a privately owned duchy of the Smythe family, stretching from the Long Island Sound to Islip and from Huntington to Setauket. Richard "Bull" Smythe, so-called because of his purported proclivity for bull riding, obtained the land from the Gardiner family (of Gardiner's Island) in 1663. Tradition has it that the western boundary of the property was established by Smythe's agreement with the Matinecock Indians of the north shore that in exchange for some (unknown) consideration, Smythe would be allowed all the land he could circumscribe in one day's bull riding. The legend is commemorated in the famous bronze bull monument at the intersection of Routes 25 and 25A in Smithtown.

The terrain of eastern Smithtown and the Nissequogue Peninsula varies from wooded hills to the beachfront of Long Island Sound and wetlands of the Nissequogue River. This is a relatively difficult ride, however, since all the roads in the area, while very scenic, are narrow, shoulderless, and offer little forward visibility. The ride starts from the Village of the Branch and proceeds north on North Country Road (Route 25A). This is a gradual uphill climb with appreciable traffic but with a wide shoulder. Off North Country Road, at the end of Harbor Hill Road at Moriches Road, is the St. James General Store and Drug Museum. The store has been at this location since 1857 and offers an assortment of handcrafted knickknacks.

Proceeding north on Moriches Road, which is shoulderless and quite narrow, we enter the village of Nissequogue, passing fine old Victorian and colonial homes in a semirural setting, with stretches of farmland and open fields. Nissequogue was probably the most desirable of the Smythe family holdings since it was here that the original Smythe homestead was established. On the right is the Old Nissequogue School, built in 1808 by seven members of the Smythe clan and one Peter Jayne.

How to get there: Exit 56 on the Long Island Expressway, north on Route 111 for about 4 miles to Route 25, Main Street-Middle Country Road, Village of the Branch. Park in any of the parking lots at the intersection.

DIRECTIONS FOR THE RIDE:

- Start from any of the parking lots at the intersection of Route 111 and Main Street-Middle Country Road (Route 25) in Village of the Branch.
- Proceed north across Middle Country Road, bearing right past the Smithtown Library onto Route 25A, North Country Road.
- Continue on North Country Road for about 2 3/4 miles, past Sts. Philip and James Church, and St. James Episcopal Church to Harbor Hill Road on the left.
- Left on Harbor Hill Road one block to Moriches Road and the General Store.
- Left on Morisches Road for about 3 miles to Horse Race Lane, passing the Old Nissequogue School and the Smythe family cemetery on the right. Follow Horse Race Lane for about 1 mile to Short Beach. (About 1/2 mile past the schoolhouse is Long Beach Road on the right, a 5 1/2 -mile round-trip to Long Beach Park on the Nissequogue Peninsula.)
- Return from Short Beach on Horse Race Lane to Nissequogue River Road on the right, opposite the Smythe family cemetery.
- Right on Nissequogue River Road for about 3 1/4 mile to Middle Country Road and Route 111, the ride starting point.

Just past the schoolhouse is Long Beach Road, a 5 1/2-mile run through beautifully wooded land dotted with attractive homes and several horse farms. This peninsula is said to have been the headquarters location of the Nissequogue Indians, the original owners of the land. It was later farmed successfully by the earliest Smythe family settlers and their descendants. Along the way is Long Beach Town Park on Long Island Sound. At the peninsula's end is a private yacht club from which you can enjoy an excellent view of Stony Brook Harbor.

Just past Long Beach Road is the Smythe family cemetery, on the right opposite Nissequogue River Road. The small plot, set back about 200 feet from the road on a dirt trail, contains the graves of Richard Smythe and his wife Sara. From the cemetery we proceed north on Horse Race Lane to Short Beach Town Park, past which the Nissequogue River empties into Long Island Sound. There is swimming available on wide pleasant beaches, and a small snack shop offers sandwiches, coffee, hot dogs, and other goodies. The approach to the beach offers an excellent view of the Nissequogue River. The shores are tidal flats in which a large variety of waterfowl and marsh vegetation can be seen. Across the way are the buildings of the King's Park State Hospital.

From Short Beach we return to the Smythe family cemetery and turn south on Nissequogue River Road. All along the way on this rather hilly but scenic road are well-tended, spacious, and attractive homes. On the right bordering the road is the gradually narrowing Nissequogue River.

At the end of this leg we come back to the ride starting point in the Village of the Branch. It is interesting to explore on foot the Colonial homes and buildings that have been maintained in the village. These include the Caleb Smith House (c. 1819) on North Country Road just past the Smithtown Library; the Homestead House (c. 1768) and Epenitus Smith Tavern (c. 1750) just east of the library; the Smithtown Presbyterian Church (c. 1750) opposite the library; and the Old School House (c. 1802) on Singer Avenue south of Main Street. At the intersection of North Country Road and Nissequogue River Road is the Smithtown Cemetery, in which many Smythe family descendants are buried.

10. Stony Brook — Port Jefferson

Number of miles: 17 (11 without Port Jefferson segment)
Approximate pedaling time: 4 hours (3 hours without Port
    Jefferson segment)
Terrain: Hilly
Surface: Generally good; some sections rough surfaced and sandy
Traffic: Heavy on Route 25A, light to moderate elsewhere
Things to see: Old Stone Lighthouse, Melville Memorial Park,
    Brewster House, Port Jefferson Harbor, Thompson House,
    Barn Complex, Stony Brook museums

Stony Brook, Setauket, and Port Jefferson are old colonial communities dating from the mid-1600s, when Setauket, settled by New Englanders, became the first community in what was to become the town of Brookhaven. The area remains as it must have been then — wooded hills, scenic and inviting harbors, and permeating it all a feeling of prosperity and comfort. The ride begins at Stony Brook Harbor, proceeds east through Setauket and Port Jefferson, and returns to Stony Brook. It is recommended that some additional time be alloted at the end of the ride to allow for a stroll through the interesting museum complex at Stony Brook.

We leave Stony Brook and head for Old Field Point. Christian Avenue is a long uphill climb along which are interesting colonial-style homes on pleasant, tree-shaded grounds. On Quaker Path the surroundings become more rural and the trees and houses larger. Finally, on Old Field Road we go through an area of extremely attractive homes on spacious and well-tended acres. At Old Field Point, from the edge of a sand cliff that drops off steeply to the water, we obtain a grand view of Long Island Sound with Connecticut in the distance. To the right is the Old Stone Lighthouse, built in 1868, now a private residence.

Returning to Old Field Road we see Conscience Bay on the left, presenting a serene waterscape complete with substantial bayside homes and attractive sailboats gliding lazily along. Further on we come to the village of Setauket. This is the oldest village in the area and once served as the seat of local government. Its importance lay in its location at the head of Conscience Bay at the confluence of two streams that entered the bay at this point. As in so many other

How to get there: East from Northern State Parkway on Route 454 to Route 347 (Nesconset Highway) to Nicoll's Road. North on Nicoll's Road to North Country Road (Route 25A), then west on 25A to Main Street, Stony Brook. Right on Main Street to the parking area at Stony Brook Harbor near the Three Village Inn.

DIRECTIONS FOR THE RIDE:

- Start from the parking area at Stony Brook Harbor near the Three Village Inn.
- Proceed around the circle onto Main, then left onto Christian Avenue, heading east past the Stony Brook Craft Center.
- Continue on Christian Avenue for about 1 3/4 miles to Quaker Path.
- Left on Quaker Path for about 1 mile to Old Field Road.
- Left on Old Field Road for about 2 miles to Old Field Point.
- Return from Old Field Point about 3 1/2 miles on Old Field Road onto Main Street in Setauket, to Route 25A.
- Left on Route 25A for about 3 1/2 miles to Main Street (Route 112) in Port Jefferson.
- Right on Main Street 1/4 mile to Liberty Avenue on the right.
- Right on Liberty Avenue one block, then straight ahead onto Old Post Road for about 2 miles to its end at Gnarled Hollow Road.
- Right on Gnarled Hollow Road about 1/4 mile to Route 25A.
- Left on 25A for about 1/4 mile to Main Street on the right.
- Right on Main Street to Melville Memorial Park at the head of Conscience Bay.
- Continue on Main Street and North Country Road, left at the bridge, back to 25A.
- Right on Route 25A for about 3 1/2 miles to Main Street in Stony Brook, near the museums at Stony Brook complex.
- Right on Main Street about 1/2 mile back to the ride starting point at the parking area at Stony Brook Harbor near the Three Village Inn.

places, the mills set up on the streams became the center of commerce and public activity. At the head of Conscience Bay currently is Melville Memorial Park, containing an upper and lower mill pond and an old mill and post office.

At the end of Main Street in Setauket we come to heavily trafficked Route 25A, which we follow all the way to Port Jefferson. On the left, three blocks from Main Street on Runs Road, is the Brewster House, a restored early-eighteenth-century home. At the end of the long downhill run is the waterfront area of Port Jefferson, a place completely different in pace from the serenity of Setauket and Stony Brook. Here all is hustle and bustle, with heavy traffic and crowded streets. Autos and people depart for Bridgeport, Connecticut, on ferries leaving from the foot of Main Street. Boat horns sound and motorboats roar. This contrast must always have existed since from its earliest days Port Jefferson was an important north-shore harbor. It was an early center of shipbuilding and a landing from which cordwood, taken from the pine and oak barrens to the south in the middle of the island, was shipped to New York. On Prospect Street is the Port Jefferson Historical Society Museum, in which mementos of the village's vibrant past are displayed.

We return toward Setauket on Old Post Road, past the Sherwood-Jayne House, built around 1730, in which can be seen antique home furnishings and craft items. We continue west on Route 25A to Main Street, which loops north to Conscience Bay from 25A at this point and then returns south to North Country Road. On North Country Road is the Thompson House, an early-eighteenth-century farm house, currently the headquarters of the Society for the Preservation of Long Island Antiquities. Just north of this is the Barn Complex, a restored eighteenth-century barn displaying typical farming equipment of the time.

We continue south on North Country Road to 25A, then west (right) on 25A past the Stony Brook railroad station, out to Main Street in Stony Brook. You can walk the remaining 1/2 mile to better peruse the museums at Stony Brook.

11. Wading River

Number of miles: 18 (9 miles without farm segment)
Approximate pedaling time: 4 hours
Terrain: Hilly near Wading River and shore, flat elsewhere
Surface: Generally good; some sections rough surfaced and sandy
Traffic: Light to moderate
Things to see: Wading River, Shoreham Nuclear Power Plant,
    Miller Homestead, Wildwood State Park

Long Island was shaped by ancient glaciers that scoured New England and scraped out Long Island Sound. The most visible remains of this action are the sand cliffs bordering the sound from Port Jefferson to Orient Point and the hilly moraines that line the island along its north shore and middle. The hills provided the most attractive areas for settlements, and their loamy soil proved excellent for farming. This ride explores one of the oldest of such communities and goes through farmlands that lie on the gentle slopes back from the edges of the cliffs.

The ride begins at Wildwood State Park and proceeds onto North Wading River Road, heading west toward Wading River. The road is quite hilly and at points may have to be walked. It is attractive, however, lined with heavy woods and neat, comfortable-looking homes. We turn north on North Side Road just past the Little Flower Institute, a Catholic home for orphaned and disadvantaged children, and continue on hilly terrain to Sound Road and Wading River Beach.

At the beach we can see the sand cliffs stretching away in both directions and the giant boulders deposited here and there by the glaciers. The cliffs are imposing but fragile, with sections unprotected by vegetative cover gradually being eaten away by the action of tides and storms. Directly behind Creek Road, lined with beachfront cottages, are the flat and marshy Wading River wetlands. The river itself can be seen at the end of Creek Road, emptying into Long Island Sound. There is a boat-launching ramp here and usually a good deal of activity as fishermen and water-skiers come and go. The river at low flow is a slow-moving, shallow trickle; after heavy rains, however, it's a swift, strong stream. Just beyond the river is the

How to get there: Exit 68 on the Long Island Expressway north on William Floyd Parkway, following signs to Wading River. Exit parkway on Route 25A; proceed east about 4 miles, following signs to Wildwood State Park.

DIRECTIONS FOR THE RIDE:

- From the Wildwood State Park parking lot, proceed west toward Wading River on North Wading River Road about 1 3/4 miles to North Side Road, just past Little Flower Institute.
- Right on North Side Road about 1 mile to Sound Road.
- Right on Sound Road to Wading River Town Beach.
- From Wading River Beach continue on Creek Road to its end at the Wading River outlet on Long Island Sound.
- Return on Creek Road to Sound Road, then right on Sound Road for about 1/2 mile to North Country Road in the town of Wading River.
- Left through the town past the Historical Society, Congregational Church, and Miller Homestead on North Country Road for about 1 1/4 miles, to the intersection with Sound Avenue and Route 25A. Note that North Country Road goes left at Wading River Manor Road.
- Proceed left on Sound Avenue about 3 1/2 miles to Edwards Avenue.
- Right on Edwards Avenue about 2 miles to Route 25, Middle Country Road. Be prepared for a steep hill and gully at Baiting Hollow.
- Right on Route 25 about 3 miles, bearing right onto Route 25A. Follow signs to Wildwood State Park, until you reach Hulse Landing Road.
- Right on Hulse Landing Road about 2 miles to Wildwood State Park and the ride starting point.

Long Island Lighting Company's Shoreham electric generating plant, an atomic-powered facility that has permanently altered the rustic atmosphere of the area. The plant has been under construction since the early '70s and has been the subject of claim and counterclaim by power advocates and environmentalists for an even longer time. Present indications are that it will not be allowed to operate. This would be a victory with nationwide significance for antinuclear groups.

From here the ride proceeds up Sound Road to the village of Wading River, which dates from earliest colonial times. The village prospered as a small farming center for most of its history, but perhaps because of its somewhat remote location, it never grew to any appreciable size. Except for the auto traffic and the few small new buildings at its center, it probably looks much as it did in its earliest days. At the western edge of the village at North Country and Gabriel Mills roads is the Wading River Historical Society headquarters, a restored early-nineteenth-century house. Further east on North Wading River Road is the Wading River Congregational Church, built around 1830, replacing the original meeting house built in 1740. At the intersection of North Wading River Road and North Country Road is the Miller Homestead, a brown weathered structure built in 1797.

We proceed south from Wading River on North Country Road to Sound Avenue and the beginning of a 6-mile run through pleasant rolling farmland. It comes as a surprise to most people to learn that Suffolk County, usually thought of as part of the New York megalopolis, is the leading agricultural county in New York State. A recent U.S. Agricultural Census indicates that Suffolk County was first in the state in agricultural income, flower growing, number of nurseries, acreage of sod, potato production, output of ducks, number of acres irrigated, and number of large farms. It was second in the growth of strawberries. The local produce can be sampled at the farm stands along Sound Avenue.

At the end of Edwards Avenue we head back toward Wildwood Park on Route 25. There is usually some traffic here, but the road has a wide shoulder. We turn north on Hulse Landing Road back to the park. Wildwood Park offers a pleasant beach, refreshments and rest rooms, and roads and paths from which cyclists can observe the good life in outdoor and vehicle camping.

12. Riverhead

Number of miles: 20
Approximate pedaling time: 4 hours
Terrain: Flat with some hilly stretches on the north shore
Surface: Good; some sandy sections
Traffic: Heavy in Riverhead, light to moderate elsewhere
Things to see: Suffolk County Government Center, Pier Avenue
Beach, Sound Avenue, Jamesport Town Beach, Suffolk
County Historical Society Museum

This is a long but easy ride through the varied neighborhoods of the town of Riverhead. The area is the most heavily urbanized in eastern Long Island, containing a mix of industrial and commercial activity and farming. As in most places on Long Island, the sea is not far away—in addition to its developed sections, Riverhead has its share of attractive beachfronts on Long Island Sound and Great Peconic Bay.

The ride starts from Riverhead on the Peconic River. The original English settlers appeared here in 1690, after which the village grew slowly into a major commercial center, capitalizing on its strategic location at the head of Peconic Bay and both forks. One of its most important activities today is as the county seat of Suffolk. About 1/2 mile west of the ride starting point, on the south side of the river, is the Suffolk County Government Center, an imposing display of governmental architecture.

We progress north on the Northville Turnpike along a stretch of bland residential buildings and flat scrubland. About 2 miles out, however, we begin to get a view of the more hilly and attractive farmlands of the north section of the area. After crossing Route 105, a four-lane speedway connecting the north and south forks, we come to Sound Avenue and Penny's Road.

Continuing north on Penney's Road we come to Sound Shore Road, on which we head east along a heavily wooded crest overlooking beautiful farms south, and, visible through the trees here and there, Long Island Sound to the north. About a mile along we come to a fuel-oil tank farm consisting of a collection of huge oil-storage tanks painted an inconspicuous green. It is apparent that efforts have been made here to minimize the visual blight, but nonetheless it

How to get there: From the Riverhead exit on the Long Island Expressway, proceed east on Route 25, following signs to Riverhead. Continue on Route 25 (Main Street) to Peconic Avenue in central Riverhead. Park in the municipal parking lot on Peconic Avenue.

DIRECTIONS FOR THE RIDE:

- Start from the municipal parking lot on Peconic Avenue in River-head.
- Right onto Peconic Avenue from the parking lot to East Main Street (Route 25).
- Jog right on East Main to the first left, Roanoke Avenue (County Road 73).
- Left on Roanoke four blocks to Northville Turnpike (County Road 43) just past the railroad tracks.
- ,Right on Northville Turnpike about 3 1/2 miles to Sound Avenue, crossing County Road 58 and Route 105.
- Jog right on Sound Avenue to Penney's Road on the left.
- Left on Penney's Road about 1/2 mile to its end at Sound Shore Road.
- Right on Sound Shore Road past the tank farm, about 2 1/2 miles to its end at Pier Avenue.
- Left on Pier Avenue to the beach on Long Island Sound.
- Return on Pier Avenue about 1/2 mile to Sound Avenue.
- Left on Sound Avenue about 1 1/2 miles to Aldrich Lane.
- Right on Aldrich Lane about 1 1/2 miles to Route 25 (going right at Franklinville Road).
- Right on Route 25 about 1/4 mile to Laurel Lane on the left.
- Left on Laurel Lane about 3/4 mile to Peconic Bay Boulevard.
- Right on Peconic Bay Boulevard about 4 1/2 miles to its end at Meeting House Creek Boulevard.
- Right on Meeting House Creek Boulevard to Hubbard Avenue, just past the railroad tracks.
- Left on Hubbard Avenue about 2 miles to East Main Street in Riverhead.
- Left on East Main Street about 1 mile to Peconic Avenue in central Riverhead.
- Left on Peconic Avenue to the ride starting point in the municipal parking lot.

remains an eyesore. The problem extends to the waterside also, where from the beach at the end of Pier Avenue can be seen the off-shore loading platform of the tank farm, and at times, the tankers unloading their cargo.

From the beach at Pier Avenue we head south back to Sound Avenue, then east, then south again on Aldrich Lane. This 3-mile leg is the very antithesis of the oil-storage tank farm and of industrialization in general. In sharp contrast to the first part of the ride, we are brought back to a different age and lifestyle in the rich, quiet, green, and bountiful farms of the area. Descriptions of Sound Avenue dating from the 1800s portray a scene much like that seen today along this unique road. It remains one of the most attractive country roads in the New York City vicinity.

At the end of this segment we go south on Laurel Lane to the shore of the north fork on Great Peconic Bay. We head west on Peconic Bay Boulevard, with farmland to the north and vacation homes on pleasant narrow lanes running to the bay to the south. About 1 1/2 miles along we come to the Jamesport Town Beach at which you can swim and obtain refreshments if you wish. It offers an excellent view of the bay, across which the Shinnecock Hills of the south fork can be seen. The pleasant scenery of Peconic Bay Boulevard continues for about 3 miles to the village of Aquebogue. From here we continue for about 2 miles, paralleling the railroad tracks along Hubbard Avenue back into Riverhead on East Main Street.

Main Street, of course, offers many eating places and the opportunity to browse around a busy downtown shopping area. For something quieter you might try the Suffolk County Historical Society Museum about two blocks west on Main Street at Osborn Avenue. It displays interesting artifacts of three centuries of Suffolk County history.

13. Mattituck—Cutchogue

Number of miles: 15
Approximate pedaling time: 3 hours
Terrain: Flat
Surface: Good; sandy in places
Traffic: Light except for Route 25, which can be heavy
Things to see: Octagonal Building, Mattituck Inlet, Cutchogue
  Village Green museum complex, New Suffolk village,
  Mattituck Airport

Mattituck and Cutchogue are two of the oldest communities in the town of Southold, both dating from around 1650. They are located on sites of former Indian villages, Cutchogue being named after a tribe that controlled most of the land in the area. Mattituck Inlet, at the head of which sits Mattituck Village, runs 2 miles into the north fork from Long Island Sound and is the only harbor on the 50-mile or so stretch between Port Jefferson and Orient Point. Cutchogue faces Little Peconic Bay to the south. Both villages were farming centers, collecting the produce of the productive farms that surround them. Mattituck especially was known for its fruits and vegetables, particularly its great quantities of strawberries. During the last ten years it has also become a center of grape growing and wine making—new agricultural activities for Long Island. Although the farming character of the land remains, it is fast being changed as more and more vacationing people travel through the area and as the land is converted from farming to residential use.

The ride starts from Mattituck where at the intersection of Love Lane and Route 25, on the left, is an octagonal building, an architectural shape quite popular on Long Island in the 1800s. We turn right here and head west on Sound Avenue, over the railroad tracks and, further on, County Route 48 onto Cox Neck Road. This is a quiet rural road that passes through farmland and patches of scrub oak. Further on, on Breakwater Road, is the open farmland that once covered the entire area. Coming in on the left are the roads of communities of homes built in the last twenty years.

At the end of Breakwater Road we come to Mattituck Inlet on Long Island Sound. The inlet itself consists of parallel rock jetties, 150 feet apart, forming a channel for the swift-moving inlet stream.

How to get there: East 10 miles from the end of the
Long Island Expressway at Riverhead on Route 25,
through Aquebogue, Jamesport, and Laurel to Mattituck. Left on Love Lane, off Route 25 just past the
Mattituck Presbyterian Church. Park in the railroad
parking lot one block north of Love Lane.

DIRECTIONS FOR THE RIDE:

- From Love Lane, Mattituck, proceed south to the Route 25 intersection and then right on Sound Avenue. The octagonal building is on the left.
- Continue for 1 mile on Sound Avenue to County Route 48 (also known as County Road 27 and Route 27A).
- Cross County Route 48 and proceed on Cox Neck Road for about 3/4 mile to Breakwater Road (Luthers Road further on) on the left.
- Left on Breakwater Road about 1 1/4 miles to its end at Mattituck Inlet.
- Return to Naugles Drive, the first road on the left.
- Left on Naugles Drive about 1/4 mile to its end at Mill Road.
- Right on Mill Road about 1 mile, continuing on to Cox Neck Road.
- Continue on Cox Neck Road about 1/4 mile to Westphalia Road on the left.
- Left on Westphalia Road about 1 1/4 miles to County Route 48.
- Left on County Route 48 to Love Lane.
- Right on Love Lane past the ride starting point to Route 25.
- Left on Route 25 about 2 3/4 miles to Cases Lane in Cutchogue. Along the way on the right, near Cardinal Drive, is the Mattituck Historical Society Museum.
- Right on Cases Lane past the Old House, Old Schoolhouse, and the Wickham Farmhouse, to its end at Cedar Road.
- Left on Cedar Road through the Cedar Golf Club to New Suffolk Road.
- Right on New Suffolk Road 1 1/4 miles to Main Street, New Suffolk.
- Left on Main Street to First Street, then right to the beach and return.
- Continue west on Main Street, then New Suffolk Avenue, 3 miles back to main road, Route 25, Mattituck, passing Mattituck Airport at Airway Drive on the left opposite Marratooka Pond.
- Right on Route 25 at Mattituck Presbyterian Church to the ride starting point on Love Lane.

Directly behind the beach can be seen vacation homes that are very much in demand because of their view of Long Island Sound and the relatively short travel time to New York City.

We return to Mattituck through pleasant farm country on Mill Road and proceed onto Westphalia Road, an older residential area bordering Mattituck Creek. At the intersection of Westphalia and County Route 48 is a good view of the head of Mattituck Creek and one of its quiet arms, comfortably harboring sailboats, outboards, and other small craft.

From Mattituck we head east toward Cutchogue on heavily trafficked Route 25. On the right, about a mile along at Cardinal Drive, is the Mattituck Historical Society Museum. The building is a restored house built originally around 1800. In Cutchogue we turn right on Cases Lane and come to a cluster of historic buildings on the Cutchogue Village Green. On the left is the Old House, built in 1649, and on the right, the Old Schoolhouse Museum, built around 1850. Also on the right is the William Wickham House, an early American home built in the 1740s. The buildings are worth seeing for their collections of colonial and postcolonial furnishings and artifacts.

We proceed south from the Village Green to New Suffolk on Little Peconic Bay. This community dates from the mid-1800s when its beautiful bayside location was first developed as a summer vacation area. From the beach at the end of First Street is a view of Robbins Island to the south and Little Hog Neck and Nassau Point to the east. A sign on Main Street notes that this was the location of the Holland Submarine Company, which was in business for a while here at the turn of the century.

We return to Mattituck on New Suffolk Road with Great Peconic Bay on the left. This road crosses extremely attractive tidelands and passes a number of beautiful homes along the bay. Just before reaching Mattituck we pass Marratooka Pond on the right, around which are several attractive homes. On the left, at Airway Drive, is the entrance to Mattituck Airport, where small private aircraft can be perused close up. At Route 25 is historic Mattituck Presbyterian Church, an imposing colonial struture, and beyond that the ride starting point at Love Lane.

14. Southold — Bayview

Number of miles: 14
Approximate pedaling time: 3 hours
Terrain: Moderately hilly
Surface: Good; sandy in places
Traffic: Heavy in Southold, light elsewhere
Things to see: Southold Burying Ground, Custer Institute,
     Horton Point Town Park and Museum, Hashamomuck
     Beach, Thomas Moore House

Southold shares with Southampton the distinction of being the oldest English settlement on Long Island. Settlers first arrived in 1640, having encamped first in New Haven, across Long Island Sound in Connecticut. Their names — Youngs, Horton, Ackerly, Wells, Corey — are echoed in the names of the streets and avenues of the present village of Southold and the peninsula of Bayview. They were hard workers and staunch Puritans, for many years allowing only members of the church to share in the civil authority of the community. The discipline and fortitude of the founders and their descendants caused Southold to become early on one of the most successful farming communities on Long Island. The town of Southold is still a prosperous farm area, and the village of Southold at its center exhibits a small-town coziness only partly offset by the heavy traffic of summer visitors.

The ride proceeds from the village of Southold south through Bayview, or Great Hog Neck, to Southold Bay and Little Peconic Bay, then north back through Southold to Horton Point on Long Island Sound, then back to Southold. It provides a good mix of farming and nautical environments, blended with a comfortable historical ambience.

Proceeding west on Main Street (Route 25), we pass on the left the First Presbyterian Church of Southold and the Southold Burying Ground. The church building was erected in 1803, but predecessors date from 1640 when it was organized as the First Church Congregation of Southold. A marker notes that the church burying ground is the oldest English burying ground in New York State. As we continue onto Bayview Road we come to the New York State Archaeological Society Museum, which displays Long Island

77

How to get there: Go approximately 17 miles east of Riverhead on Route 25 to the town of Southold. Park in the bank parking lot off Youngs Avenue on the north side of the road.

DIRECTIONS FOR THE RIDE:

- Start from the bank parking lot off Youngs Avenue on Route 25, Southold. Proceed out onto Route 25 (Main Street) and right (west) for about 1 mile past the First Presbyterian Church on the left to Bayview Road on the left fork, just past Jockey Creek Drive on the left and Ackerly Pond Lane on the right.
- Follow Bayview Road for about 3 miles to its end at Cedar Beach Road, passing the Archaeological Museum and Custer Institute, and further on at Cedar Lane, the Abijah Corey House.
- Left on Cedar Beach Road about 1/2 mile to Cedar Beach.
- Returning from Cedar Beach, take the first right onto Paradise Point Road for about 1/2 mile to North Bayview Road (unmarked).
- Left on North Bayview Road for about 1 mile to Jacobs Lane on the left. Go right here, continuing on North Bayview Road for about 1 3/4 miles, over the Goose Creek Bridge, to its end at Pine Neck Road.
- Left on Pine Neck Road about 1/2 mile to Oaklawn Avenue on the right.
- Right on Oaklawn Avenue, over the bridge, to its end at Route 25 (Main Street).
- Jog right on Route 25; then turn left onto Horton Lane.
- Continue on Horton Lane, across Route 27A, about 1 1/2 miles to Soundview Avenue.
- Right on Soundview Avenue to Lighthouse Road.
- Left on Lighthouse Road to Horton Point Town Park and Museum.
- From Horton Point return on the first left, Soundview Avenue Extension, to Soundview Avenue.
- Continue left on Soundview Avenue for about 1 1/2 miles to the intersection with Route 27A near Hashamomuck Beach.
- From the beach go right (west) on 27A about 1 1/4 miles to Boisseau Avenue and the turnoff to Southold.
- Follow the Southold sign left onto Boisseau Avenue and continue on for 3/4 mile over the railroad tracks to Route 25, Main Street, Southold.
- Right on Route 25 past the Thomas Moore House and the Southold Historical Society Museum to the bank parking lot off Youngs Avenue.

Indian artifacts, pottery, and sculpture. Directly opposite it is the Custer Institute with its domed observatory. The institute is the home of a private astronomy study group that maintains the observatory and its equipment. It's open to the public at various times during the summer.

Further south on Main-Bayview Road, just north of Cedar Lane is the Abijah Corey House, built in the early 1700s. It shows its age and contrasts sharply with the modern homes that surround it. As we continue on Main-Bayview Road we turn left at the General Wayne Inn, an excellent restaurant, and come to Cedar Beach at the end of Cedar Beach Road. This is a 1/4-mile pebbly beach on Little Peconic Bay providing no amenities but offering unsupervised swimming and a good view of the bay. Just back of the beach is a concrete structure housing the Suffolk County Community College Marine Science Center. From here we continue on North Bayview Road and leave Bayview on the Goose Creek Bridge. There is a great view of Southold Bay to the east and Goose Creek, a pleasant tranquil backwater, to the west.

We proceed back through Southold and then north on Horton Lane, a sparsely developed area of farms and flat woodlands, onto Sound View Avenue and Lighthouse Road to Horton Point Town Park and Museum. The lighthouse at the park dates from 1857. At the end of Lighthouse Road is a stair leading to the beach on Long Island Sound. Stairs of this type, common all along the cliffs of the north shore, often require rebuilding as erosion eats the soft cliffs away. From the top of the stair is an unobstructed view of Connecticut on the horizon.

Going east on Sound View Avenue, on rather hilly terrain, we pass through a heavily treed stretch (which unfortunately blocks the sound view) and come to Hashamomuck Beach on Long Island Sound. This is a long, wide beach providing swimming, refreshments, and rest rooms. It is flanked by hotels and motels and is usually frequented by a good-sized crowd. We return to Southold on Boisseau Avenue and come to the Thomas Moore House on the south side of Route 25. This structure was built prior to 1658 and has recently been restored. Further on, at Maple Lane, is the Southold Historical Society Museum, a cluster of four buildings displaying antique home decorations, toys, tools, carriages, and other items.

15. Greenport — Orient Point

Number of miles: 21
Approximate pedaling time: 4 hours
Terrain: Flat
Surface: Good; sandy in places
Traffic: Heavy in Greenport, light to moderate elsewhere
Things to see: East Marion Orient Park beach, Orient Point
Ferry landing, Orient village, Greenport

This ride explores the eastern tip of the north fork from Greenport to Orient Point. It runs on a narrow peninsula never more than 1 1/2 miles wide. At points, only a few hundred feet of sandy soil separate Long Island Sound on the north from Orient Harbor on the south. This ride provides the most striking example of the mingled farm and sea environments of eastern Long Island. At times the feel and tang of the sea predominate, but this can change suddenly to an air of earthy farmland as one passes by fertile and ripe fields. It is an experience that is available to cyclists in few other places and makes this a most pleasant ride.

The ride starts from the Long Island Railroad parking lot adjacent to the Shelter Island ferry slip in Greenport. Proceeding east we go past the Island's End Golf and Country Club through East Marion and continue on about 2 miles to the narrowest section of the peninsula, with Orient Harbor on the right and tranquil Dam Pond on the left. Orient Harbor presents an attractive waterscape, with the tip of Orient Beach State Park straight ahead and the village of Orient to the left. A half mile further on is the East Marion Orient Park, with its long stretches of inviting Long Island Sound beach.

We continue on Route 25 all the way to the end of the north fork. This entire stretch is becoming more heavily developed and trafficked on the Long Island Sound side as vacation homes and condominiums rise along the water's edge. At the end of Route 25 we find the Orient Point Ferry to New London, Connecticut, and just west of this is a modern private marina where meals and snacks are served. The ferries come almost to the beach in a narrow crude slip where they discharge vehicles and passengers through openings at their ends.

How to get there: East about 25 miles from Riverhead on Route 25. On approaching Greenport, follow signs to the Shelter Island Ferry. Park in the Long Island Railroad parking lot adjacent to the ferry landing at Third and Wiggins streets.

DIRECTIONS FOR THE RIDE:

- Start from the railroad station parking lot at Wiggins and Third streets, Greenport.
- Proceed onto Third Street and then up one block to Front Street.
- Right on Front Street to its end at Main Street.
- Left on Main Street, following signs to 25 East, about 3/4 mile to Route 25 (Main Road).
- Right (east) on Route 25 for about 8 miles to its end at the Orient Point Ferry. East Marion Orient Park Beach is on the left, halfway along.
- Return on Route 25 for about 2 1/2 miles to Narrow River Road on the left.
- Left on Narrow River Road for about 2 miles, bearing left at the Narrow River Mariner, halfway along, to its end at King Street.
- Right on King Street about 1 mile to Village Lane.
- Right on Village Lane through Orient Village Historic District, for about 1 mile, to its end at Route 25.
- Left (west) on Route 25 for about 5 miles to Main Street, Greenport.
- Left on Main Street through the Greenport shopping area, to its end at Front Street.
- Right on Front Street to Third Street.
- Left on Third Street to Wiggins Street and the ride starting point at the railroad parking lot.

Also at Orient Point is the departure point for the United States Department of Agriculture Plum Island facility. Plum Island, 2 miles out in Long Island Sound, is the site of extensive investigation of animal diseases, many of which are highly contagious. Great care is taken to control all contact with the labs, hence the tall fences around the docks. A quarter mile west of here is the entrance to the Orient Beach State Park. There is a narrow road that runs for about 2 miles to the park beach, providing a great view of Gardiners Bay to the south and narrow Little Bay to the north, the latter filled with marsh grass teeming with seabirds.

We return toward Greenport on Route 25, turning off at Narrow River Road into the village of Orient. This community dates from the mid-1600s when the earliest Southold settlers arrived. The village contains a number of interesting historic structures, including the Shaw House (c. 1730), the Orient Point School House (c. 1888), the Oysterponds Historical Society Museum (four buildings c. 1790 to 1890), the Orient Methodist Church (c. 1835), and the Webb House Museum (c. 1740). All of these are clustered on Village Road. Orient has maintained its small-town coziness and is a most pleasant place for cycling.

We continue west from Orient on Route 25, turning south at the sign for Greenport. The railroad reached Greenport in 1844, at which time the town was just beginning to grow. It supported a small whaling fleet and several menhaden fish-processing plants — evil-smelling operations that provided fish oil and fertilizers. Hopes that a major link with New England would be formed with the railroad and ferry service never quite panned out, and the village grew slowly to its present size.

The Greenport shopping area, specifically Front and Main streets, is worth visiting. It contains a number of boutiques, bookshops, and art galleries. At the foot of Main Street is Preston's, a ship chandlery that offers every conceivable type of marine hardware, clothing, and equipment, and a large selection of books, ship models, and nautical paintings. Further north on Main, between Adams and South streets, is the Sterling Historical Society of Greenport Museum.

16. Shelter Island

Number of miles: Basic ride — 18; southern loop — 5; western
    loop — 7; total — 30
Approximate pedaling time: Basic ride — 4 hours; southern loop-
    1 hour; western loop — 2 hours; total — 7 hours
Terrain: Hilly in northern sections, flat elsewhere
Surface: Good; some sections rough surfaced and sandy
Traffic: Moderate on Route 114, light elsewhere
Things to see: Shelter Island Ferry, Ram Island Drive, Osprey
    nests, Sylvester Manor Windmill, Crescent Beach

Shelter Island is a 4-by-6-mile, randomly shaped plug located between Long Island's north and south forks, almost connecting the
two. It faces Peconic Bay to the west and Gardiners Bay to the east,
with narrow channels separating it from Greenport on the north and
North Haven on the south. It is generally hilly but contains beautiful
wooded areas, usually associated with the north shore of Long Island, and miles of beaches and superb water views. Except for the
main north-south road, Route 114, it has little traffic, and there are
no sections of the island that would be considered heavily developed.
It is, in fact, a very quiet and conservative community. The population of about 1,700 people increases in the summer, but not exces-
sively, and it contains few amusements beyond the extremely
attractive scenery of water, woods, and homes. Even its history is
somewhat subdued compared to the rich variety of neighboring
Southold and the Hamptons. Not much remains of its colonial past
in the way of structures and historical items, perhaps because the island has always been sparsely populated. For the cyclist, however, it
is a perfect place for a day's outing especially when the pleasant ferry
rides are added to the experience.

   The ride consists of three parts: the basic ride covering the
north central part of the island; a loop through the western parts;
and a loop through the southern parts. The basic ride assumes the
rider has come from Greenport; those coming from the south — from
North Haven and Sag Harbor — can pick up the ride route through
the southern loop.

   After leaving the ferry from Greenport we proceed into Shelter Island Heights and immediately come to the hills that are

How to get there: From the north fork: ferry from Greenport, 25 miles east of Riverhead on Route 25. Park in the Long Island Railroad parking lot, adjacent to the ferry at Greenport. From the south fork: ferry from North Haven, 24 miles east of Riverhead on Routes 27 and 79. Limited parking is available near the ferry landing at the end of Route 114 in North Haven.

GARDNERS BAY

N

GARDNERS BAY DRIVE

LOCK

DINERS BAY C.C.

S LA.

ISLAND RD.

RAM ISLAND DRIVE

LITTLE RAM ISLAND DR.

COECLES

RAMS INN

N. RAM ISLAND

S. RAM ISLAND

RAM ISLAND

INLET

CH

0   ½   1 MILE

FERRY HAVEN HARBOR

DIRECTIONS FOR THE RIDE:

- From the ferry landing at Summerfield Road, follow Route 114 South on Grand and Chase avenues over Chase Creek to Winthrop Road on the left.
- Continue on Winthrop Road, with Dering Harbor on the left, over Gardiner Creek to the village of Dering Harbor, just past Cobbetts Lane.
- Go right onto Locust Point Road, and continue on for about 1/2 mile to Sylvester Road, just past the Dering Harbor Town Hall.
- Right on Sylvester Road for several hundred yards, then right again at the road entrance to the Gardiners Bay Country Club on the left.
- Left through the club on Dinah Rock Road to the traffic circle, then left, continuing on Dinah Rock Road.
- Continue on Dinah Rock Road for about 2 miles to Ram Island Drive (Dinah Rock becomes Gardiners Bay Drive about a quarter of the way along.)
- Proceed out to Ram Island and return on Ram Island, North Ram Island, and South Ram Island drives, about 6 miles round-trip.
- From Ram Island, turn left at Gardiners Bay Drive, continuing on Ram Island Road for about 1 1/4 miles to the traffic circle.
- Left at the circle onto St. Mary's Road, then on for about 1/2 mile to Ferry Road, Route 114.
- Right on 114 past the Shelter Island Presbyterian Church, then straight ahead halfway around the circle onto Bateman Road.
- Continue on Bateman to Midway Road.
- Right on Midway about 1/2 mile to Bowditch Road on the left.
- Left on Bowditch to its end at Menantic Road at the Shelter Island Racquet Club.
- Right on Menantic over West Neck Road (Route 28), onto New York Avenue, with the Shelter Island Country Club on the left.
- Continue for about 1/2 mile on New York Avenue past Tower Hill Road to Grand Avenue.
- Bear right on Grand Avenue and continue for 1/2 mile to Summerfield Road and the ride starting point at the North Ferry.

Western Loop:

- From the Menantic-West Neck Road (Route 28) intersection, proceed west on West Neck onto Shore Road (Route 42), then on for 1 1/4 miles to its end at Nostrand Parkway. Crescent Beach is on the right.

- Follow Nostrand Parkway (Brander Parkway further on) for 1 1/2 miles to Lilliput Lane on the right.
- Right on Lilliput Lane to its end at Peconic Avenue.
- Left on Peconic Avenue for about 1 mile to North Brander Parkway.
- Left on North Brander, continuing onto Brander Parkway.
- Continue on Brander Parkway for about 1 mile to West Neck Road on the right, opposite Bootleggers Alley.
- Right on West Neck Road to its end at Shore Road.
- Right on Shore Road 1/4 mile, connecting with the basic ride at Menantic Road.

Southern Loop:
- From St. Mary's Road, continue south on Ferry Road (Route 114), for about 2 miles to its end at the south ferry landing, passing Havens House on the right.
- Return on Ferry Road for about 1 mile to Midway Road on the left.
- Left on Midway for about 2 miles, connecting with the basic ride at Bateman Road.

found in the northern part of the island. This area is a melange of new and old homes, some dating from Victorian times, as evidenced by the gingerbread facades and busy architecture of the older homes along Grand Avenue. We proceed through this area, probably the busiest on the island, and arrive at Chase Creek. Here we get the first of the several excellent views of the intricate harbors and inlets that exist on all sides of the island. To the north is Dering Harbor, with the Shelter Island Yacht Club on the left. Behind is Chase Creek, a typically quiet and serene backwater. Further on we cross Gardiner Creek, with much the same view, and arrive at the village of Dering Harbor.

Dering Harbor is a community of expensive, well-tended homes shaded by massive trees, with terrific views of Dering Harbor, Shelter Island Sound, and Greenport. We pass through this attractive area and come to a more modern community at Dinah Rock Road, after traversing Gardiners Bay Country Club with its clipped fairways and greens. The homes along Dinah Rock are spaced wider apart and are lower and more rambling than those seen previously, but they remain quite attractive and maintain the water view. Many of the crossroads go to the water's edge, from which a broader view can be obtained.

At Ram Island Drive we come to a narrow 3-mile-long peninsula jutting into Gardiners Bay, encircling Coecles Harbor. Along this stretch we see in microcosm all the attributes of Shelter Island: treed and hilly terrain, pebbly, wind-blown beaches, and attractive homes. At the intersection of North and South Ram Island drives is the Rams Inn, an old, well-known lodging place. You will note on the stretches along the beaches the large stick-and-twig nests located on platforms on sawed-off utility poles. These are used by ospreys, beautiful birds reaching up to 3 feet in wingspan, that were once abundant here and in similar places on Long Island. Sometime in the past, however, they began to decrease in number, reportedly because of the effects of chemical pollutants in their food supply. However, the latest Audubon Society bird counts indicate that more of them are surviving, lending hope that they will again populate the area to the extent they once did.

From Ram Island Drive we head inland to the center of the island on hilly terrain. On Manwaring Road, just west of Ram Island Road, is the Sylvester Manor Windmill, built around 1800. Just south is St. Mary's Episcopal Church on the left. We turn west on Ferry Road and proceed to the center of the original Shelter Island settlement.

The first settlers arrived in 1652. By 1674, after a complicated series of sales, ownership of the island rested entirely with Nathaniel Sylvester. The island was then subdivided several times, so that by 1730 ownership was spread among its twenty male inhabitants. It changed very slowly in the next two centuries, its population not exceeding 1,000 until the early 1920s. The site of the original settlement now contains a Presbyterian Church, founded in 1742, with the present building surrounded by cemeteries containing the graves of the early residents. From the village center we head west to Midway Road and then north on Menantic Road, back to Shelter Island Heights and the road back to the ferry.

The western loop begins where Menantic Road meets West Neck Road. We proceed west on Shore Road past Crescent Beach, a public swimming area with a beautiful water view, and proceed onto Nostrand Parkway. Along this leg and south on Peconic Avenue are some of the most attractive houses on Shelter Island. Some are new and of quite interesting designs; others are large, comfortable, old weather-beaten structures. All command a striking view of Shelter Island Sound, and in the distance, Great Hog Neck. The way back goes past West Neck Bay, with more of the same comfortable and quiet scenery.

The southern loop starts from Ferry Road at the intersection with St. Mary's Road. We proceed south on Route 114 through an area of heavy woods and in some spots some commercial buildings and stores. About a mile along we come to Haven House, the former residence of the Havens family. It was built in the mid-1700s and is now maintained by the Shelter Island Historical Society. Continuing down Ferry Road we come to its end at the landing of the North Haven ferry. As in most other places on the island, the view of the racing water, passing boats, and shoreline homes is stunning. We proceed north on Midway Road from Ferry Road, passing the Shelter Island Town Beach, looking out over Shelter Island Sound, and further on pass Menantic Creek on the left. The southern loop meets the basic ride at Bowditch Road.

17. Five Towns — Long Beach

Number of miles: 20
Approximate pedaling time: 4 hours
Terrain: Flat
Surface: Good
Traffic: Medium to heavy
Things to see: Old Gristmill Museum, Woodmere Town Dock,
    Rock Hall, Atlantic Beach and Long Beach boardwalks

This ride encircles the inlet-strewn bays between the Five Towns area bordering New York City, Atlantic Beach, and Island Park, Oceanside, and East Rockaway in southern Nassau County. There is great variation in lifestyles to observe among these communities and several interesting stops along the way.

The ride begins from Lister Park at Ocean Avenue in Rockville Center. It proceeds through the park into East Rockaway, a typical older Long Island suburban area of comfortable appearance. At the intersection of Denton and Woods avenues we come to the Old Gristmill Museum, a weathered gray building dating from 1688, since restored, that once stood on the Mill River, probably close to where Lister Park is now. It displays nineteenth-century Long Island village life and work scenes, as well as tools and implements used at the time.

About 1 3/4 miles further on, at Deering Land and Main Street begin about 6 miles of curving quiet roads bordered by large and attractive homes. This is the southern section of the Five Towns area — Hewlett, Woodmere, Cedarhurst, Inwood, and Lawrence — one of the earliest settled areas on Long Island. It is situated at the head of a peninsula that reaches down and around Jamaica Bay to the west. At one time Five Towns was heavily farmed, but with the coming of the railroad in the early 1800s it became a center for vacationers heading for the Rockaways further out on the peninsula. It is now a commuters' colony whose proximity to New York City and the bays and waterfront of the Long Island south shore make it a most desirable place to live (despite the screaming jets going into and out of Kennedy International Airport, 3 miles to the west).

Halfway along this leg, at the end on Woodmere Boulevard in Hewlett Neck, is the Woodmere Town Dock, a good resting spot providing an excellent view of Brosewere Bay and the marshy islands that are typical of the Nassau County south shore. The ride continues from here along the Woodmere Club to Keene Lane, where we cut through the Woodmere Club grounds and go through a marshy area at the head of Woodmere Channel Basin. In the early morning hours this area is alive with shorebirds of all kinds.

Further on in Lawrence, we come to Rock Hall, one of the most celebrated colonial homes on Long Island. It is an imposing Georgian-style building built in the late 1700s for Josiah Martin, a wealthy West Indies planter. It is furnished with eighteenth-century antiques which accurately re-create home decorations for this type of house when it was in active use.

From Rock Hall we proceed south over Reynolds Channel on the Atlantic Beach Bridge to the community of Atlantic Beach. Atlantic Beach, and Long Beach just east of it, extend for 5 1/2 miles on the first of the barrier beaches that border the entire south shore of Long Island. These towns were developed in the late nineteenth century as vacation and recreation areas. They are now primarily year-round residential communities, although there is still a considerable summer inflow of vacationers. The Atlantic Beach and Long Beach boardwalks are most enjoyable. From here you get an open ocean view, the opportunity for a swim and access to a number of snack shops and restaurants.

From Long Beach we go back over Reynolds Channel on the Long Beach Bridge for the 6 1/2-mile return leg to Lister Park. Just over the bridge we traverse Island Park and then proceed through Oceanside. These communities are much like East Rockaway at the beginning of the ride.

How to get there: Southern State Parkway to Exit 17 south, to Sunrise Highway via Hempstead Avenue and Ocean Avenue. Starting point is the Lister Park parking lot, 300 feet east of Ocean Avenue on the south side of Sunrise Highway, adjacent to the water tower.

DIRECTIONS FOR THE RIDE:

- Start at the Lister Park parking lot, Rockville Center.
- Proceed through Lister Park along the Mill River to the park exit at South Park Avenue.
- Right on South Park Avenue to Ocean Avenue.
- Left on Ocean Avenue 1/4 mile to Centre Avenue.
- Right on Centre Avenue, over railroad tracks, to Atlantic Avenue.
- Left on Atlantic Avenue to Woods Avenue.
- Left on Woods Avenue to Denton Avenue. The Old Gristmill Museum is at the intersection.
- Continue on Denton Avenue to Atlantic Avenue.
- Right on Atlantic Avenue 1/4 mile to merge with Main Street; continue on Main 3/4 mile to Deering Lane on the left.
- Left on Deering Lane around to Waverly Avenue.
- Left on Waverly to Everit Avenue on the right.
- Right on Everit Avenue to Everit Place.
- Right at Everit Place, continuing on Everit Avenue (the road turns, but it is still Everit Avenue) to Albon Road.
- Right at Albon Road, continuing on Everit, around Marcy Channel to Meadowview Avenue at the schoolground fence.
- Left on Meadowview Avenue about 3/4 mile to East Broadway.
- Left on East Broadway to Browers Point Branch (not Brower Avenue).
- Left on Browers Point Branch to Woodmere Boulevard; left on Woodmere Boulevard to its end at the Woodmere Town Dock.
- Out of the town dock back up Woodmere Boulevard to Ivy Hill Road on the left.
- Left on Ivy Hill Road, which becomes West Ivy Hill Road, bordering the Woodmere Club grounds to Keene Lane. The Woodmere Clubhouse is on the left.
- Left on Keene Lane through the Woodmere Club grounds to Atlantic Avenue.
- Right on Atlantic Avenue approximately 1/4 mile to the merge with Chauncey Lane on the left.
- Continue right on Chauncey Lane to the intersection with Auerbach Lane, Barret Road, Cedarhurst Avenue, and Briarwood X.
- Left at the intersection onto Barret Road to Washington Avenue on the right.
- Right on Washington Avenue to Kenridge Avenue.

- Left on Kenridge Avenue to merge with Meadow Lane.
- Continue left on Meadow, across Causeway Road, onto Rock Hall Road.
- Continue on Rock Hall Road to Lawrence Avenue.
- Right on Lawrence Avenue to Broadway. Rock Hall is on the left at the intersection.
- Left on Broadway 1/2 mile to Doughty Boulevard.
- Left on Doughty Boulevard, 1 mile, to the Atlantic Beach Bridge.
- Over the bridge to Atlantic Boulevard.
- Jog left on Atlantic Boulevard to the United Way, to Plaza.
- Right on Plaza to Ocean Boulevard.
- Left on Ocean Boulevard approximately 1 1/4 miles to its end at Yates Avenue. The Atlantic Beach Boardwalk parallels this segment and can be ridden in season.
- Left on Yates one block to Park Street.
- Right on Park Street (Beech Street further on) 1 3/4 miles to Grand Boulevard.
- Right on Grand Boulevard to the Long Beach Boardwalk.
- Left on the boardwalk 1 1/4 miles to Long Beach Boulevard.
- Off the boardwalk onto Long Beach Boulevard, then over the Long Beach Bridge, to Bridge Plaza.
- At Bridge Plaza follow the Island Park signs, continuing on Long Beach Boulevard to the left.
- Through Island Park and Barnum Island on Long Beach Road, approximately 1 3/4 miles, over the railroad tracks, to the intersection with Austin Boulevard.
- Continue on Long Beach Road to the left at Austin Boulevard intersection for approximately 1 1/4 miles to West Henrietta Avenue in Oceanside.
- Left on Henrietta to Fulton Avenue.
- Right on Fulton Avenue 3/4 mile to merge with Lincoln Avenue on the left.
- Continue right on Lincoln, across Atlantic Avenue to Woods Avenue on the left.
- Left on Woods Avenue 1 mile to the merge with Rockaway Avenue on the left.
- Continue across Rockaway Avenue onto Park Place.
- Continue on Park Place to South Park Avenue.
- Left on South Park Avenue to Hendrickson Avenue.

- Right on Hendrickson Avenue to the Lister Park entrance, then through the park back to the ride starting point.

18. Garden City

Number of miles: 15
Approximate pedaling time: 3 hours
Terrain: Flat
Surface: Good
Traffic: Moderate to heavy
Things to see: Old Nassau County Courthouse, Garden City
Hotel, Cathedral of the Incarnation, Cradle of Aviation
Museum

This ride explores communities that developed on what was known
as the Hempstead Plains a one-time treeless prairielike expanse that
stretched from what is now the Queens County border well into Suffolk County. The village of Hempstead, forming the nucleus of earliest development in the 1600s, was surrounded later by Garden City,
an exclusive residential area, Mineola, the seat of county government, and other villages to the south.

The ride starts at the quadrangle of Nassau Community College and proceeds west on Stewart Avenue into Garden City, indicated by the appearance of tree-lined streets and expensive homes.
The city was founded in the late 1800s by A. T. Stewart, a wealthy
New York merchant, and gradually became the home of other well-
to-do families. It has maintained this characteristic ever since.

The ride progresses a mile or so north toward Mineola and the
Nassau County government complex. On County Seat Drive, we pass
on the right the boxy, modern, green-glassed Supreme Court Building. Ahead and to the right is the Nassau County Court House, built
in the depression days of the 1930s. On Franklin Avenue and Old
Country Road is the Old Nassau County Courthouse, the most interesting of all the buildings in the area. It dates from 1900, when its
cornerstone was laid by Theodore Roosevelt. All around are law
offices and buildings servicing the local legal and political industry.

Going back to Garden City on Hilton Avenue we pass through
an area of charming old homes that face the Garden City Hotel, a
new structure replacing the original hotel, which was the very center of Garden City social life for more than fifty years. Immediately
to the west is the imposing spire of the Cathedral of the Incarnation,
constructed in 1876 by the widow of A. T. Stewart. North of

How to get there: Exit M3 on Meadowbrook Parkway, west on Stewart Avenue 1/2 mile to Selfridge Avenue on the left. Left on Selfridge Avenue to Nassau Community College. Park in the lot adjacent to the college quadrangle.

DIRECTIONS FOR THE RIDE:

- Left from Selfridge Avenue on Stewart Avenue to Wetherill Road.
- Right on Wetherill Road to Kingsbury Road.
- Left on Kingsbury Road, to Washington Avenue, then jog left to Eleventh Street on the right.
- Right on Eleventh Street to County Seat Drive.
- Right on County Seat Drive to Old Country Road.
- Left on Old Country Road to Franklin Avenue.
- Left on Franklin Avenue to Fourteenth Street.
- Right on Fourteenth Street to Golf Club Lane.
- Left on Golf Club Lane to Eleventh Street.
- Right on Eleventh Street to the intersection with Hilton and Cherry Valley avenues.
- Sharp left on Hilton Avenue to Sixth Street.
- Right on Sixth Street to Cathedral Avenue.
- Right on Cathedral Avenue to the intersection with Cherry Valley and Stewart avenues.
- Left on Stewart Avenue to Rockaway Avenue.
- Right on Rockaway Avenue to the Merillon Avenue fork.
- Proceed on Merillon Avenue (left fork) to Oxford Boulevard.
- Left on Oxford Boulevard to Newmarket Road.
- Right on Newmarket Road 1 mile to Tanners Pond Road.
- Left on Tanners Pond Road to Stewart Avenue.
- Left on Stewart Avenue to Nassau Boulevard.
- Right on Nassau Boulevard to Cambridge Avenue.
- Left on Cambridge Avenue about 1 mile to Cherry Valley Avenue and First Street.
- Jog left on First Street to Rockaway Avenue.
- Left on Rockaway Avenue one block to Second Street.
- Right on Second Street to Franklin Avenue, then across to Main Street. Proceed on Main Street one block to Meadow Street.
- Left on Meadow Street to Lindbergh Street.
- Right on Lindbergh Street to Westbury Boulevard.
- Left on Westbury Boulevard to Oak Street.
- Right on Oak Street to Hempstead Turnpike.
- Left on Hempstead Turnpike to Uniondale Avenue.
- Left to Nassau Community College, the ride starting point.

the church, at the intersection of Stewart and Rockaway avenues, is Saint Paul's School, part of the cathedral complex.

The next 5 miles of the ride is a pleasant tour through the residential western reaches of Garden City, and then past the Garden City Country Club, the Adelphi University campus, and the Cherry Valley Country Club, all exhibiting quiet vistas of green grass and trees. East of here we continue for about 3 miles through more modest but still attracitve residential areas, until we reach the western edge of Old Mitchel Field at Hempstead Turnpike and Oak Street. On Hempstead Turnpike is Hofstra University, with its main facilities and library on the right and its dormitories, looming like Easter Island colossi, on the left. At Uniondale Avenue the ride goes north, back toward Nassau Community College.

In the early years of the century, the area encompassing Mitchel Field and Roosevelt Field to the north was the site of extensive aviation experimentation and development. Glenn Curtiss flew here as early as 1909. The area featured numerous tournaments and aviation exhibitions, eventually becoming a general aviation center. In 1927 Roosevelt Field served as the departure point for Lindbergh's famed solo flight across the Atlantic. Flying activities became more restricted as the surrounding areas developed after World War II. The last planes flew from Mitchel Field, by then an Air Force Base, in 1961. Artifacts of the activity are available for viewing at the Cradle of Aviation Museum at Mitchel Field. On display are restored aircraft of early Long Island aviation pioneers and the World War II period, and modern jet aircraft and spacecraft built on Long Island. It is a most interesting museum and well worth a stop.

As we head north through the area we pass the Nassau County Veterans Memorial Coliseum on the right, opened in 1972, offering professional sporting events, entertainment, and shows and exhibitions of all kinds. Straight ahead is the Nassau County Community College, the starting point of the ride.

19. Freeport — Seaford

Number of miles: 16
Approximate pedaling time: 3 hours
Terrain: Flat
Surface: Good
Traffic: Usually heavy, but light on Sunday mornings
Things to see: Wantagh Park, Mill Pond Park, Cammanns Pond
  Park, Freeport Historical Society Museum, Woodcleft Canal,
  Tackapausha Museum and Preserve.

This ride explores a section of Merrick Road that runs through the
towns of Freeport, Merrick, Bellmore, Wantagh, and Seaford —
names that make up part of the conductor's litany on the Long Island Railroad's south-shore line. These were originally isolated
bay-oriented villages connected by a passable but difficult Merrick
Road. However, in the 1800s and early 1900s the railroad spurred
their development by providing fast, easy access from Brooklyn and
New York. Land developers and the railroad itself widely advertised
the attractions of the area, inducing thousands of New Yorkers to
leave the city and settle in this new suburb. Improvement of Sunrise
Highway and Merrick Road continued the trend through the
postwar years, leading to the current state of saturation.

The ride proceeds west from Wantagh Park on Merrick Road
along a popular shopping strip connecting Wantagh, Bellmore, and
Merrick. For 2 1/2 miles there are antique shops, clothing stores, restaurants, and fast-food outlets. There are also several ponds and
parks along the way, including Mill Pond Park in Wantagh, a wide,
quiet body of water harboring hundreds of ducks and geese, and
Cammanns Pond Park in Merrick. The ride turns left at Cammanns
Park and follows the attractive, long, tree-lined pond to Shore Drive,
which circuits a peninsula jutting into Merrick Bay. The peninsula
is typical of development that has taken place in the last twenty years.
The houses are attractive and expensive but close-packed, blocking
all public access to the bay and eliminating wetlands along the shore.

The ride proceeds from here over the Meadowbrook Parkway
into Freeport. This is the oldest of the communities along the
stretch and the most heavily populated. Just north of the ride route
is the center of the town with its busy bustling streets filled with shop-
pers. Upon entering Freeport, the ride goes left at Mill Road

How to get there: Exit W6 on Wantagh State Parkway onto Merrick Road, to Wantagh Park, immediately west of the Parkway. Signs indicate the way to the park.

DIRECTIONS FOR THE RIDE:

- Start at Wantagh Park parking lot.
- Out of Wantagh Park on bicycle-path exit to Bayport Court.
- Jog left on Bayport to Woodland Avenue.
- Right on Woodland to Merrick Road.
- Left on Merrick Road for 2 3/4 miles to Lindenmere Drive on the left, just before Cammanns Pond Park in Merrick.
- Left on Lindenmere Drive to Shore Drive.
- Right on Shore Drive around the Clubhouse Road, to Bernard Street, then left at Bernard, continuing on Clubhouse Road to Merrick Road.
- Left on Merrick Road over Meadowbrook Parkway to Mill Road in Freeport. Mill Road is the left fork just past the overpass.
- Left on Mill Road for 1/2 mile to intersection with South Main Street.
- Left on South Main to Freeport Historical Society Museum, then on to Atlantic Avenue.
- Right on Atlantic for about 1/2 mile to South Grove Street.
- Left on South Grove past Randall Park to Front Street.
- Right on Front one block to Woodcleft Avenue.
- Left on Woodcleft Avenue along Woodcleft Canal.
- Return to Wantagh retracing the way along Woodcleft, Front, South Grove, Atlantic, South Main, Mill Road, and Merrick Road.
- To return to starting point, go right on Woodland to Bayport Court and the Wantagh Park bike path. For the Seaford leg, continue on Merrick Road for about 2 miles past Woodland Avenue, to Washington Avenue in Seaford. Signs indicate the approach to Tackapausha Preserve.
- Left on Washington Avenue to Tackapausha Preserve and Museum.
- From the museum, turn left back to Merrick Road.
- Right on Merrick Road to Woodland Avenue, then left to Bayport Court and the Wantagh Park bike path and ride starting point.

and heads for the waterfront district. On South Main Street is the Freeport Historical Society Museum. This pleasant little building displays artifacts of local history and Civil War memorabilia.

From here we proceed to the Woodcleft Canal, Freeport's "Nautical Mile," on which is a collection of boat dealers and builders, ship chandlers, commercial and charter fishing boats, fish dealers, seafood restaurants, and a smattering of shops dealing in nautical bric-a-brac. Opposite the canal are small cozy houses adding a homey touch to the whole scene. The end of the canal provides a great view of the bay and the private yachts and commercial fishing boats of the area. In summer, the street is usually crowded with strollers and autos for its entire length. There is a lot to see, and it's a great place for lunch.

Upon returning to Wantagh, we continue on for 2 miles to Seaford. This village has retained its nautical bent along Merrick Road, despite the residential development it has experienced over the years. On Washington Avenue is the Tackapausha Museum and Preserve. The museum displays samples of local fauna and flora in their natural habitat; the preserve consists of 80 acres of different types of vegetation common on Long Island.

At the end of the ride, Wantagh Park itself has about 2 miles of bike paths, extensive playgrounds and picnicking facilities, a snack bar, and rest rooms. The family dramas that occur on the boat-launching ramp are always interesting to watch, and the boat basin has dozens of pretty, small boats and a fine water view.

20. West Hills

Number of miles: 9 (13 with Old Bethpage Village side trip)
Approximate pedaling time: 2 hours (3 with Old Bethpage Village
   side trip)
Terrain: Hilly
Surface: Generally good; some rough and potholed sections
Traffic: Heavy on Round Swamp Road, moderate elsewhere
Things to see: Suffolk County West Hills Park, Old Bethpage
   Village Restoration, historic homesteads along Chichester
   and West Hills roads

This ride explores an area in transition — a one-time bucolic area that
evolved into an archetypical Long Island suburb. The area is unique,
however, in that it contains visible elements of this entire evolution
within an extremely small geographic area. Along the 9 miles or so
of the ride we pass vividly contrasting sights, including colonial
homes, newly built (or still-under-construction) commercial com-
plexes, farms, and suburban housing tracts. It is a challenging but interesting tour.

The ride begins at the Suffolk County West Hills Park on Sweet
Hollow Road. We proceed south from here on Sweet Hollow Road
to the town of Melville. Sweet Hollow Road is a beautiful, heavily
wooded stretch that shows little of the surrounding suburban
development. It is narrow and shoulderless, however, and has some
traffic.

At Melville we turn south (right) along Walt Whitman Road,
passing along the way a series of ultramodern glass-and-concrete
buildings housing many of the companies that have prospered in this
part of Long Island. Route 110, just east of Walt Whitman Road, has
become Long Island's premier high-tech corridor, the site of end-
less building (and traffic) and the incubator of dozens of electronics,
communications, and computer companies. It is the showcase of the
extremely high-powered economic growth of Long Island in the last
decade.

At Cottontail Road the ride turns west into Manetto Hills and
proceeds for about 2 miles through an extremely attractive area of
spacious homes, clipped lawns, and manicured shrubbery. You will
note immediately that Hills is an appropriate designation for this
area.

How to get there: Long Island Expressway exit 49N, Route 110. North on Route 110 to Old Country Road. Left (west) on Old Country Road 1/4 mile to Sweet Hollow Road. Right (north) on Sweet Hollow Road 1/2 mile to Suffolk County West Hills Park.

DIRECTIONS FOR THE RIDE:

- Left (south) from West Hills Park on Sweet Hollow Road 1 mile, past Old Country Road, to Walt Whitman Road.
- Right on Walt Whitman Road 1/2 mile to Cottontail Road on the right, just before the Expressway.
- Right on Cottontail Road 1 mile to East Mall Drive.
- Left on East Mall Drive to Bensin Drive.
- Left on Bensin Drive to Old Country Road.
- Left on Old Country Road a short distance to Round Swamp Road. (The ride continues to the right, but for a visit to Old Bethpage Village, turn left (south) and continue for about 2 miles to the village entrance on the left.)
- Right on Round Swamp Road for 2 miles, passing under the Northern State Parkway, to High Hold Drive on the right.
- Right on High Hold Drive to its end at Mt. Misery Road.
- Left on Mt. Misery Road 1/4 mile to Chichester Road.
- Right on Chichester Road 1 mile, staying right at the Sweet Hollow Road intersection, to West Hills Road.
- Left on West Hills Road one block to Downs Road.
- Left on Downs Road 1/4 mile to Sweet Hollow Road.
- Left on Sweet Hollow Road 1 mile to West Hills Park, the ride starting point.

After winding through Manetto Hills we arrive at Old Country Road, a major east-west artery, for a short run to Round Swamp Road. Along Old Country Road, in contrast to the suburban setting just toured, are operating farms where, in season, bikers can rest and sample the local produce.

The ride proceeds north (right) from Old Country Road at this point, but for those with the time and the inclination, it is worth a trip south on Round Swamp Road to the Old Bethpage Village Restoration, located about 1 1/2 miles from Old Country Road. This Nassau County facility re-creates activities, farms, houses and other buildings, shops, and crafts typical of Long Island in the mid-1800s. It also has an extensive display of books and replica artifacts for sale and a reasonably priced restaurant.

Proceeding north from Old Country Road on Round Swamp Road we pass large, newly built homes on both sides of the road for about 2 miles. this stretch is flat but is usually heavily trafficked, so cycle with care. After passing under the Northern State Parkway overpass we come to High Hold Drive on the right.

At this point the ride proceeds through an area whose architecture, roads, and greenery send us back in time to the colonial and Civil War eras. From this point on the roads are narrow (just enough room for two passing autos), hilly, curvy, and bumpy. The overall feel, however, is one of slow-paced homey comfort and quiet – in stark contrast to the beginning parts of the ride. It also has the attraction of being the childhood neighborhood of Walt Whitman, the celebrated nineteenth-century poet, author of *Leaves of Grass*.

High Hold Drive, presenting an immediate hill-climbing challenge, proceeds for about a mile through heavily wooded growth to its end at (aptly named) Mt. Misery Road. Turning left on Mt. Misery Road we come to the Conyer House on the right, dating from 1819, which was built by Walt Whitman, Sr., father of the author. Continuing on for a short distance we come to Chichester Road, named for a resident colonial family. Turning onto Chichester Road we come to the original Chichester homestead (c. 1678), used for a time as a hotel known as the Peace and Plenty Inn, and now a private residence.

At West Hills Road the ride passes a cluster of colonial buildings, including three built by the Whitman family: the Joseph

Whitman House, the Whitman—Carll house, and the Whitman-Whitehouse, all built around 1690 by forebearers of Walt Whitman. The birthplace of Whitman himself (born 1819) is a short distance east on West Hills Road, on Walt Whitman Road near Route 110.

The ride continues from West Hills Road onto Downs Road, another scenic stretch that passes a large horse farm and stables, several small old homes and cottages, and ends (after a hill climb) at Sweet Hollow Road. We stay on narrow and scenic Sweet Hollow Road for about 2 miles back to the ride starting point at West Hills Park.

21. Great River — Oakdale

Number of miles: Great River — 9; Oakdale — 4
Approximate pedaling time: Great River — 2 hours; Oakdale —
    1 hour
Terrain: Flat
Surface: Good; sandy in places
Traffic: Light
Things to see: Connetquot River, Timber Point Park, Heckscher
    State Park, Bayard Cutting Arboretum, Dowling College,
    Artists' Colony Historic District

The ride consists of two separate segments: the first through Great
River on the west bank of the Connetquot, the second through the
Idle Hour section of Oakdale on the east bank. Although it is possible to cover the entire course continuously, doing so would require
cycling on an extremely dangerous length of Montauk Highway at
the head of the river. It is recommended, therefore, that first Great
River, then Oakdale be cycled, with the trip between the starting
points done by automobile.

    The Great River segment begins from the river access road
near Timber Point Park. Immediately ahead is the Connetquot River
flowing gently to Nicoll Bay. The Connetquot meanders south from
the middle of Long Island, starting as a small stream but eventually
widening into one of the largest and most attractive rivers on the island. Directly south is the Timber Point County Park, where we see
a handsome columned clubhouse surrounded by neatly clipped and
tended fairways and greens. You can ride down to the west and east
marinas in the park for a close-up view of some of the beautiful craft
that ply the river. From the rear of the clubhouse is an expansive view
over the course and the bay.

    From Timber Point Park we proceed to Heckscher State Park,
one of several major state parks on Long Island. It contains a bicycle
path through a couple of miles of wooded picnic areas and
playgrounds to a bathing area on Great South Bay. On summer
weekends the park is quite crowded, and the cyclist must be wary of
pedestrians, especially young children.

    From Heckscher Park we go on through a modern housing
development to the Bayard Cutting Arboretum. The arboretum is a

How to get there: Exit 45 East on Heckscher State Parkway, east one block on South Country Road (Route 27A) to Great River Road. South on Great River Road about 1 1/2 miles to the river access road on the left near Timber Point Park.

DIRECTIONS FOR THE RIDE:

- Park on the side street running to the Connetquot River just north of Timber Point County Park.
- Proceed into and around the park and return to River Road.
- Left on River Road for about 1/2 mile to the merge with Timber Point Road.
- Continue on Timber Point Road to the Heckscher State Park pedestrian and bicycle entrance on the left, just past Heckscher Parkway.
- Proceed onto and around the park back to the Timber Point Road entrance.
- Left on Timber Point Road about 1/4 mile to Country Village Lane.
- Right on Country Village Lane about 1/2 mile to its end at Overlook Drive.
- Left on Overlook Drive about 1/2 mile to Route 27A.
- Right at 27A, following a pedestrian walk under the Parkway overpass, then on for about 1/2 mile to the Bayard Cutting Arboretum.
- Return on 27A from the arboretum to Great River Road.
- Left on Great River Road about 1 1/2 miles to the ride starting point.
- For the Oakdale segment, drive east on 27A past the merge with Route 27, and on 1/4 mile or so past the railroad tracks to Idle Hour Boulevard. Parking is usually available in the store parking areas on Montauk Highway.
- Go south on Idle Hour Boulevard through Dowling College on the right, about 1/2 mile to Shore Drive.
- Left on Shore Drive to Hollywood Drive.
- Right on Hollywood Drive, continuing right at Jade Street past the Artists' Colony barn to Idle Hour Boulevard at Tower Mews.
- Right on Idle Hour Boulevard to Middlesex Avenue.
- Left on Middlesex Avenue with a short jog right at Grassmen Avenue to Shore Drive.
- Left on Shore Drive for about 1 3/4 miles to its end at Vanderbilt Boulevard.
- Left on Vanderbilt Boulevard about 1 1/4 miles to Montauk Highway, then left to the ride starting point.

walkers' park—bicycles must be left at a rack at the entrance. There are five walks in the park, each devoted to a different type of vegetation and wildlife—pine tree, wildflower, rhododendron, swamp cypress, and a bird-watchers' walk—the latter two bordering on the Connetquot. The arboretum was originally owned by the family of William Bayard Cutting and was later presented as a gift to New York State. From the arboretum we proceed back on Great River Road to the starting point of the Great River Loop.

The second segment of the ride begins at Route 27A near Idle Hour Boulevard in Oakdale. The area is known as Idle Hour from the name of an old estate located here and once owned by William Vanderbilt. It's a pleasant little knot of intersecting streets and lanes lined with attractive and comfortable homes. No attempt is made here to map out in detail the maze of streets. Suffice it to say that the community is quite small and that all roads lead back eventually to Shore Drive at its perimeter.

A half mile or so in on Idle Hour Boulevard is Dowling College, the main building of which is the former Vanderbilt mansion. It was built in 1902, and its 110 rooms, extensive stone and woodwork, and palatial appearance have made it a landmark on Long Island. From the stone steps at the rear of the mansion there is an exceptionally attractive view of the Connetquot, and one can easily picture the festive events that once took place here. The building has undergone extensive renovation and repair after a fire damaged a good deal of it in 1973.

If we turn into the maze at Shore Drive we eventually come to the original farm complex purchased by the Vanderbilts, located near Hollywood Drive. The main building is a large old rambling red-brick barn featuring a number of dormers, turrets, and interesting "eyebrow" windows in the roof. This is the centerpiece of the Artists' Colony, a picturesque cluster of dwellings that during the '20s and '30s housed a community of artists. The area has recently been declared a Historical District by the town of Islip.

We continue on Shore Drive past the homes lining the river, then over a small bridge overlooking a busy boat yard. Further on, at Vanderbilt Boulevard, we can reach the water's edge and obtain one last good view before proceeding north to the ride starting point at Montauk Highway.

22. Lake Ronkonkoma

Number of miles: 14 (10 without MacArthur Airport)
Approximate pedaling time: 2 hours (1 1/2 without MacArthur
    Airport)
Terrain: Flat
Surface: Generally good; some rough sections
Traffic: Medium
Things to see: Lake Ronkonkoma, St. Joseph's Roman Catholic
    Church, Islip MacArthur Airport, Ronkonkoma Beach

Lake Ronkonkoma lies in the middle of a wide swath of land known
as the Pine Barrens, which runs east along the centerline of Long Island to the north and south forks. In colonial times and up to the last
quarter of the nineteenth century, this flat interior of Suffolk County was largely ignored while the more fertile and attractive north and
south shores were farmed and settled. Scrub oak and pine
predominated in the thin sandy soil, and it wasn't until well after the
advance of the Long Island Railroad that some interest in the area
developed. The villages and towns along the tracks grew slowly and
remained quiet country communities until the end of World War II.
Since that time, with the construction of the Long Island Expressway,
there has been a virtual explosion of development throughout the
barrens, providing moderately priced housing for thousands of ex-
city dwellers.

    The ride starts from Smith Haven Mall, a large regional shop-
ping center that services communities for miles around. It proceeds
south from the mall's south exit through about 2 miles of comfortable housing developments to the north shore of Lake Ronkonkoma.

    Lake Ronkonkoma is a large kettlehole, a gouge left by a
retreating glacier thousands of years ago. It provided a convenient
watering spot in the otherwise arid pine barrens and for half a century was a popular summer resort. However, as the sound and south-
shore beaches became more accessible and the surrounding area
developed, the lake gradually lost its appeal for vacationers. Traces
of its former use can been seen in the large old summer homes that
still remain here and there on Lake Shore Road on the east side of
the lake. The lake is still attractive, however, and provides a depar-

How to get there: From the end of Northern State Parkway go east for 1 3/4 miles on Route 454 (Veterans Memorial Highway) to Route 347 (Nesconset Highway). Continue on 347 for 5 3/4 miles to Smith Haven Mall on the right.

DIRECTIONS FOR THE RIDE:

- Follow Bike Route signs out of Smith Haven Mall onto Middle Country Road (Route 25) one block to Alexander Avenue.
- Left on Alexander Avenue to Glenfield Lane.
- Right on Glenfield Lane, continuing onto Shenandoah Boulevard, to Brown's Road.
- Left on Brown's Road one block to the continuation of Shenandoah Boulevard.
- Right on Shenandoah Boulevard to Nichols Road.
- Right on Nichols Road to Gibbs Pond Road.
- Left on Gibbs Pond Road to Steuben Boulevard.
- Left on Steuben Boulevard onto Lillian Drive to its end at Smithtown Boulevard.
- Left on Smithtown Boulevard, which becomes Lake Shore Road, around the east side of the lake about 1 3/4 miles to the intersection with Church Street, Pond Road, and Rosevale Avenue.
- Left on Church Street past St. Joseph's Roman Catholic Church to Church Street Extension, then left again to continuation of Church Street, to Ronkonkoma Avenue.
- Right on Ronkonkoma Avenue about 3/4 mile over the Long Island Expressway and the Long Island Railroad tracks onto Smithtown Avenue.
- Continue for about 1 1/2 miles on Smithtown Avenue, with Islip MacArthur Airport on the left, to Lakeland Avenue.
- Right on Lakeland Avenue 1/4 mile, past 15th Street, to Pond Road.
- Right on Pond Road for 2 miles over the railroad tracks and under the Long Island Expressway back to the Church-Pond-Rosevale intersection.
- Left on Rosevale Avenue about 1 1/2 miles, past Ronkonkoma Beach at Kirk Avenue, to its end at Smithtown Boulevard.
- Right on Smithtown Boulevard for about 1/4 mile to Lillian Drive, then left to Steuben Boulevard.
- Follow Steuben, Gibbs Pond, Nichols, Shenandoah, Brown's, Shenandoah, Glenfield, Alexander, and Middle Country roads back to Smith Haven Mall and the ride starting point.

ture from the ocean and bay water views usually associated with Long Island.

At the south end of the lake, at Lake Shore Road and Church Street, is St. Joseph's Roman Catholic Church. The church complex consists of several buildings, including an old and new school, a convent, a church, and a rectory. The older school and convent, built of stone, date from the 1920s; the new school, church, and rectory, built of brick with stylized adornments, date from the mid-'50s and '60s. Together they provide an interesting contrast in architectural design over the forty-year period.

Continuing south on Ronkonkoma Avenue we pass over the Long Island Expressway and then over a narrow two-lane bridge over Long Island Railroad tracks. Ronkonkoma Avenue becomes Smithtown Avenue at this point, and within two heavily industrialized blocks we come to Islip MacArthur Airport. This is a commercial field providing jet service to cities along the northeastern seaboard of the United States. Air traffic is becoming heavier as Suffolk County grows, and the field has become a major transportation center for Long Island. Along Smithtown Avenue, however, are the flight schools, charter services, and air taxis that were at one time the prime users of the field. You can cycle near the parking strips and hangars of these operations and observe the aircraft up close.

We return to Lake Ronkonkoma on Pond Road through a light commercial and rural stretch and then continue north on the west side of the lake on Rosevale Avenue. Opposite Kirk Avenue is Ronkonkoma Beach. It features a bathhouse, swimming area, playground, and tennis and handball courts. It's a good place to stop for a rest and snack.

From Ronkonkoma Beach the route progresses onto Smithtown Boulevard around to the north side of the lake, then back to Smith Haven Mall and the ride starting point.

23. Smith Point

Number of miles: 9
Approximate pedaling time: 2 hours
Terrain: Flat
Surface: Smooth but sandy; one dirt-road section
Traffic: Light to moderate
Things to see: Pattersquash Creek, Manor of St. George Museum, Brookhaven Town Beach, Smith Point

This is a pleasant ride that offers the opportunity to see the variety of water views, wetlands, and ocean beaches that abound on the south shore of Long Island. The Mastic peninsula juts into the southern bay, separating the bay into its major sections: Great South Bay to the west and Moriches Bay to the east. Due south from Smith Point, the southern tip of the peninsula, is Fire Island Beach and the open Atlantic.

The peninsula has an interesting colonial past dating from the late seventeenth century, when William Smith of Northampshire, England, at one time governor of Tangiers, and later the holder of varied posts in the New York colonial government and militia, purchased from the local Patchogue Indian tribe a large tract of land running from the Connetquot River in the west to the Farge River in the east, and north to the middle of the island. The patent issued for this purchase also included the Strong Neck peninsula just east of the village of Setauket on the north shore. Mastic was the birthplace of William Floyd, delegate to the first Continental Congress and later one of the signers of the Declaration of Independence, and of Nathaniel Woodhull, who participated in the French and Indian War as a member of the New York colonial army and who later commanded a brigade of Suffolk and Queens county militiamen in the American Revolution. A touch of the past remains in the Manor of St. George Museum in the village of Shirley.

The ride starts from the east side of the William Floyd Parkway near the Smith Point Bridge tollbooths and proceeds north on the parkway to Baybright Drive. Although the parkway has wide smooth shoulders, it is sometimes heavily trafficked and should be cycled with care. As we head east on Baybright and Elm and then south on Cranberry Road, we go through typical housing developments

How to get there: Exit 68 on the Long Island Expressway, or the Shirley exit on Sunrise Highway (Route 27), south on William Floyd Parkway to the approach to the Smith Point Bridge. Turn left from William Floyd on the last exit before the toll and park on a local side street near the tollbooths on the east side of the road.

DIRECTIONS FOR THE RIDE:

- Start from the parking area near the tollbooths on the east side of William Floyd Parkway.
- Proceed north on William Floyd about 1 mile to Baybright Drive.
- Right on Baybright Drive to Johns Neck Road.
- Jog left on Johns Neck Road to Elm Road on the right.
- Right on Elm Road for about 1/2 mile to Cranberry Drive.
- Right on Cranberry Drive to its end at the waterside parking area.
- Left on Riviera Drive (unmarked dirt road that tees into Cranberry Drive near the parking area).
- Continue on Riviera for about 1 1/4 miles, with Pattersquash Creek on the right, to Ducky Lane.
- Continue on Ducky Lane to Cedar Road.
- Left on Cedar Road to Bayview Drive.
- Right on Bayview Drive, past the merge with Cranberry Drive, to Neighborhood Road.
- Left on Neighborhood Road for about 1 mile to Havenwood Drive on the right, one block east of William Floyd Parkway.
- Right on Havenwood Drive, over William Floyd Parkway at the traffic light, then left one block on William Floyd Parkway to the Manor of St. George Museum.
- South from the museum on William Floyd about 1/4 mile to W. Parkview Drive.
- Right on W. Parkview Drive to its end at Grand View Drive.
- Left on Grand View Drive to Trafalgar Drive.
- Left on Trafalgar Drive back to William Floyd.
- Right on William Floyd about 1 mile, over the Smith Point Bridge, to Smith Point County Park.
- From Smith Point Park return over the bridge to the ride starting point in the parking area near the tollbooths.

that have covered the peninsula since the end of World War II. These contain modestly priced homes on small lots that have provided a haven for young families of moderate income. At the end of Cranberry Road we come to a small parking area on Narrow Bay, the strip of water that separates the peninsula from the barrier beach. To the left is Pattersquash Island, and straight ahead are the dunes of Smith Point County Park. Invariably there is a cool ocean breeze here, which, with the rich surrounding waters, makes it a popular fishing spot. Turning north we follow Riviera Drive along Pattersquash Creek. Pleasant old homes look out on the wetlands, reeds, and waters of the creek, where now and then a small sailboat or outboard goes by.

At the head of Pattersquash Creek we head west back toward William Floyd Parkway, crossing it at Havenwood Drive with the help of a traffic light, and then south a block to the Manor of St. George Museum, a stately, white colonial structure with a striking view of Great South Bay. The estate lands on which this house stands were part of the Smith purchase and were owned by the Smith family until 1954. The musuem contains papers and historical documents of the Smith family and its holdings and an outline of Fort St. George, built on the site by the British and destroyed by Americans in 1780.

From the museum we head south on William Floyd Parkway, again on a wide smooth shoulder, then west on Parkview Drive to Grand View Drive. We pass a Brookhaven Town Beach on Great South Bay, where in the late afternoon on clear summer days the bay sparkles under the setting sun.

Rejoining William Floyd Parkway at Trafalgar Drive, we head finally to the ocean beach at Smith Point County Park. There is a short run over the Smith Point Bridge, after which we come immediately to the park parking field and pavilion. Bicycling is not allowed outside the parking areas, but you can lock your bike up in any of the several bike racks and swim in the ocean breakers or just observe them from the dunes to the east and west of the parking fields. Food and refreshments are available at the pavilion. From Smith Point Park it's just a short hop back over the bridge to the ride starting point near the tollbooths.

24. Westhampton Beach — Quogue

Number of miles: 8 1/2
Approximate pedaling time: 2 hours
Terrain: Flat
Surface: Good; sandy in places
Traffic: Heavy in Westhampton Beach and village center and at
     points on Dune Road, light to moderate elsewhere
Things to see: Tiana Beach, Quogue Schoolhouse Museum,
     Quogue Presbyterian Church, Phillips Wildlife Refuge

Westhampton Beach and Quogue are the most westerly of the Long
Island southshore communities that are strung along the Atlantic
beachfront and known collectively as the Hamptons. From here east
to Montauk the vacationing is of a special kind, usually associated
with substantial wealth and gracious living, but the automobile and
road systems available to all have democratized the summer crowd
considerably.

     Westhampton and Quogue are located on separate peninsulas
that divide the south bay between the barrier beach and the island
proper into Moriches Bay to the west and Shinnecock Bay to the
east. The geography and bridgework are such that a convenient circular bicycle route is available from the villages to the ocean beaches.

     The ride starts from Westhampton and proceeds west on Main
Street, with its elegant shops and boutiques, to Potunk Lane just past
St. Marks Episcopal Church. Across the way is the Westhampton
Country Club, discreetly screened from public view. From here we
head south toward the ocean through an area of typical Hampton-
style homes and vacation retreats. The road is fairly wide, but there
is some traffic coming and going to the beaches. At the end of Jessup Lane is a bridge to the beach. It has a pedestrian way on which
you can leisurely walk your bike over the short span and enjoy the
excellent views of Moriches Bay on the right and Moneybogue Bay
on the left.

     From the end of the bridge we start a 3-mile or so ride along
the beach, heading for the return bridge at Quogue. You will note
immediately the huge beach clubs that line the road in both directions as far as the eye can see. Between the clubs are the homes that
have come to symbolize the area — fantastic shapes in wood, featur-

How to get there: Exit 63 south from Sunrise Highway (Route 27) on County Road 31 (Old Riverhead Road), past Suffolk County Airport and Montauk Highway (Route 27A), to Mill Road in the village of Westhampton Beach. Left on Mill Road to the municipal parking lot just north of the intersection of Mill Road and Main Street.

DIRECTIONS FOR THE RIDE:

- Start from the municipal parking lot at Mill Road and Main Street.
- Right on Main Street to Potunk Lane. St. Marks Episcopal Church is on the right.
- Left on Potunk Lane past Westhampton Country Club, following signs to the beach for about 1 mile on Potunk Lane, then Jessup Lane.
- Over the bridge from Jessup Lane to Dune Road on Westhampton Beach.
- Left on Dune Road for about 3 1/4 miles, past Beach Lane Bridge, to Post Lane Bridge in Quogue.
- Over the bridge halfway around the circle onto Post Lane, continuing to its end at Quogue Street.
- Right on Quogue Street to Ocean Avenue and the Quogue Museum and Library.
- Return on Quogue Street from the museum about 1 1/2 miles past the Quogue Presbyterian Chapel at Beach Lane, to Montauk Highway (Route 27A).
- Left on Montauk Highway for about 1/2 mile, over Quantuck Creek to Meetinghouse Road, diagonally opposite Strebels Laundry.
- Left on Meetinghouse Road to Main Road.
- Left on Main Road for about 1 mile, over Aspatuck Creek, to the ride starting point at Mill Road.

ing angular overhangs, dramatic arcs, circular towers, arches, spans, and every other imaginable architectural device. Some are quite interesting; others are grotesque.

It's unfortunate that this section of the road has so few public openings to the ocean itself. Amost every foot is spoken for by private homes and clubs. Ocean swimming and viewing are available from Dune Road but at some distance away from Westhampton and Quogue. About a mile west is a small public beach and, to the east, a string of beaches starting at Tiana, about 3 miles from Quogue.

We head north on Post Lane Bridge in Quogue just east of the Quogue Beach Club. Cyclists must be wary here of the often heavy traffic from the eastern beaches. As at Westhampton Beach, the water views from the bridge are excellent. At Quogue Street we turn right to the Quogue Schoolhouse Museum, one block east near Ocean Avenue. It's a weathered building built in 1822, containing artifacts and memorabilia of Quogue and Long Island.

Quogue has been a summer community since the early 1800s, and the homes seem excellently suited to this purpose. They are staid old structures, large and well shaded on spacious groomed lawns, that have about them a quality of substance and comfort. At Beach Lane is the Quogue Presbyterian Chapel, built in 1868, a neat small clapboard structure, and further on at Jessup Avenue on the right is the village center, consisting of a post office, the village hall, and several real estate offices.

We leave Quogue on Route 27A, heading west back to Westhampton. There is some traffic on this road and it's a bit hilly, but there is a wide smooth shoulder. We pass over Quantuck Creek with its complement of fishermen and to the the north observe the tranquil body of water and its surroundings — the Phillips Wildlife Refuge. We turn in from 27A on Meetinghouse Road, pass over Aspatuck Creek, and arrive back at the ride starting point at Main Street.

25. Hampton Bays — Shinnecock Canal

Number of miles: 17
Approximate pedaling time: 3 hours
Terrain: Moderately hilly in Hampton Bays; flat elsewhere
Surface: Good; sandy in places
Traffic: Heavy
Things to see: Shinnecock Canal, Ponquogue Beach, Shinnecock
  Inlet

Hampton Bays is one of the liveliest of the summer communities of Long Island's east end. Just west of the Shinnecock Canal — the narrow channel separating the Montauk peninsula from the rest of Long Island — it is in a sense the gateway to the summer playgrounds of the south fork. This ride explores this popular vacation area and the ocean beaches to which it is connected.

The ride starts from the parking area at the side of the Shinnecock Canal. From here you can see the swift-flowing stream connecting Great Peconic Bay to the north with Shinnecock Bay to the south. The canal is about 3/4 mile long and features tidal gates that control the flow of water, and a lock providing boat passage. The lock is necessary because the bays can differ in elevation by as much as 4 feet. The canal was completed in 1892, more than fifty years after it was first suggested to the state legislature.

From the canal we head north on Newtown Road, passing under Route 27, then west through a lightly developed wooded stretch at Canoe Place and Squiretown. The name Canoe Place reflects the historic Indian use of the area as a canoe portage route between the bays. Squiretown was once a center for salt-hay harvesting on Great Peconic Bay, an activity that attracted farming families from miles around during the cutting season. The terrain is fairly hilly in here, but there is little traffic, and the surroundings are attractive and quiet.

As we head south on Squiretown Road we enter Hampton Bays just south of Route 27. From here on, the atmosphere is one of a modern, busy, resort community. Most of the housing is devoted to that purpose and is in great demand, especially by singles' groups. In summer the place is crawling with sports cars, cyclists, and beach enthusiasts.

How to get there: Route 27A to the Shinnecock Canal, then north on County Road 62 (Newtown Road). Continue on Newtown Road for about 1/4 mile to Holzman Lane, the canal access road on the right just past the railroad overpass. Park at the canal side.

DIRECTIONS FOR THE RIDE:

- From the canal road, proceed left on Gate Street one block to Newtown Road.
- Right on Newtown Road, passing under Route 27, then left at the T intersection for about 1 3/4 miles to its end at Red Creek-Squiretown Road.
- Left on Red Creek-Squiretown Road about 2 3/4 miles, past Route 27, 27A, and the railroad tracks, onto Ponquogue Avenue to Bay Avenue.
- Left on Bay Avenue about 1/2 mile to Wakeman Road.
- Right on Wakeman Road to Shinnecock Road (at Penny Lane).
- Left on Shinnecock Road to Foster Avenue.
- Right on Foster Avenue about 1 1/2 miles, over Ponquogue Bridge to Beach Road and Ponquogue Beach.
- Proceed east from Ponquogue Beach about 1 mile on Beach Road to Shinnecock Inlet.
- From Shinnecock Inlet return on Beach Road past Ponquogue Beach, continuing on about 1 1/2 miles to Tiana Beach and another mile or so to "Hot Dog Beach."
- Return on Beach Road back to Ponquogue Beach, then back over the bridge to Foster Avenue, then back to Shinnecock Avenue.
- Left on Shinnecock Avenue to Wakeman Road.
- Right on Wakeman Road 1 1/2 miles to Fanning Avenue, the third right past Hampton Bays High School.
- Right on Fanning to its end at Canoe Place Road–Lynn Avenue.
- Left on Canoe Place Road to Montauk Highway, Route 27A.
- Right on 27A to County Road 62 (Newtown Road).
- Left on Newtown Road under the railroad bridge to the canal access road and the ride starting point.

South of Hampton Bays we proceed through the Ponquogue penin-sula jutting into Shinnecock Bay, and then over Ponquogue Bridge to the ocean beach. The streets leading to the bridge and the bridge itself can be quite heavily trafficked in summer as the beach crowd comes and goes. The bridge is a two-lane structure with a pedestrian walk from which you get a good view of the bay stretching to the east and west.

At the end of the bridge at Beach Road, a road that runs the length of this section of the barrier beach from Shinnecock Inlet in the east to Moriches Inlet 15 miles to the west, we come to Pon-quogue Beach, a broad stretch on the Atlantic offering swimming, rest rooms, and refreshments. If you are really hungry, however, wait until you get to Shinnecock Inlet, the next leg of the ride, where there are a number of small, salty restaurants and marinas. Shinnecock Inlet itself is a fast-flowing run providing access to the Atlantic to the boat owners on Shinnecock Bay. These small boats are usually present, fighting their way through the inlet if going against the flow or skimming in just barely under control if going with it. The inlet has existed only since 1938 when, during the great hurricane of that year, the ocean battered Long Island's south shore, cutting through the barrier beach at this point. There are usually a number of fisher-men on the rocks lining the inlet and a good crowd around the Coast Guard light.

We return from the inlet and head west past Ponquogue Beach to Tiana Beach and "Hot Dog Beach," a mile or so further on. On summer weekends these places are jammed day and night, rain or shine, with hordes of partiers, mostly of college age. The music blasts from the local bars, and the convertible and dune-buggy traffic sometimes piles up and spills onto the sand shoulders of the road. It's a bit of southern California on Long Island and a great place for a beer.

From "Hot Dog Beach" and Tiana Beach we head back over the Ponquogue Bridge back through Ponquogue on Wakeman Road, a pleasant run through the communities traversed earlier. At the end of this leg we come to Canoe Place Road-Lynn Avenue, on which we return to Montauk Highway and the canal. This road is the main north-south artery in the area and should be cycled with care.

26. Southampton — North Sea

Number of miles: 24 (12 without the North Sea segment)
Approximate pedaling time: 4 hours (2 hours without the North Sea segment)
Terrain: Flat in Southampton, hilly in North Sea segment
Surface: Good; sandy in places
Traffic: Heavy in village of Southampton, light to moderate elsewhere
Things to see: St. Andrews Dune Church, Coopers Neck Beach, Shinnecock Inlet, Bullhead Bay, Settler's Monument, Southampton Village historic architecture

Southampton, with Southold on the north fork, is one of the oldest villages on Long Island. It dates from 1640 when a band of settlers, starting from Lynn, Massachusetts, arrived at North Sea on Great Peconic Bay. With great perserverance and some shrewd real estate dealings with the Shinnecock Indian tribe, they established a thriving community resting on strict Puritan principles of sobriety and dedication to work. They selected a beautiful place, including a beachfront on the Atlantic, fertile, flat woodlands, and access to the fish and shellfish of Shinnecock and Great Peconic bays.

The ride starts on Main Street and proceeds to the eastern parts of the village at Meeting House Lane and Old Town Road. Near the center of the village the houses are large, old, comfortable dwellings, wide-spaced and shaded with massive trees. As we approach the beach the style of architecture changes to sun-bleached cedar and white trim, but the quality of comfort remains. All along Gin Lane are large and attractive beachfront homes. These line the road along the beach for most of the ride. At Agawam Lake we come to the Southampton Beach Club, a busy center of tennis and swimming, and just beyond it the St. Andrews Dune Church, built in the late 1800s, an interesting, heavy, dark-red building somewhat out of place here. Opposite it, Agawam Lake offers a neat water view that contrasts nicely with the oceanfront, being a calm, tree-lined, and generally green spot in this otherwise bright, sandy area.

About a mile along we get an opportunity to view and swim the Atlantic at Coopers Neck Beach. In addition to the breakers it offers a refreshment stand and rest rooms. Beyond Coopers Neck

How to get there: East on Route 27 on the south fork. Go south at Exit 9, North Sea Road, then follow signs to Southampton. Park in the village parking lot on the right, off Main Street.

DIRECTIONS FOR THE RIDE:

- From the village parking lot proceed right on Main Street to Meeting House Lane on the left, opposite Jobs Lane.
- Left on Meeting House Lane to Old Town Road.
- Right on Old Town Road to Gin Lane.
- Right on Gin Lane (Dune Road further on) to Meadow Lane.
- Left on Meadow Lane onto Beach Road.
- Proceed on Beach Road and return for a 4-mile round-trip along Southampton Beach.
- Left on Halsey Neck Lane (first left) opposite beach parking lot, about 1/2 mile to Boyeson Road.
- Left on Boyeson Road to Captains Neck Lane.
- Right on Captains Neck Lane to Ox Pasture Road.
- Left on Ox Pasture Road to Lee Avenue.
- Right on Lee Avenue to Hill Street, Route 27A.
- Those wishing to return to Southampton, go right on Hill Street for about 1 mile to Jobs Lane, then on to Main Street. The full ride proceeds left on Hill Street about 1 1/4 miles to Tuckahoe Road (past Tuckahoe Lane) on the right.
- Right on Tuckahoe Road through Southampton College, over the railroad tracks and Route 27 (marked Route 39) through the Shinnecock Hills Golf Club, to Sebonac Road-Barker Isle intersection.
- Proceed over Sebonac Road to Barker Isle Road, and continue on for about 1 mile to Bullhead Bay.
- Return from Bullhead Bay, then left onto Millstone Brook Road. Continue on Millstone Brook for about 1 1/4 miles, past the intersection with West Neck and North Magee roads, to Scotts Road, branching to the left from Millstone Brook.
- Continue on Scotts Road, bearing left at every intersection, to its end at North Sea Road.
- Left on North Sea Road to its end at Conscience Point Beach.
- Return on North Sea Road (Suffolk County Route 38) for about 1 1/2 miles to Route 27. (About 1/2 mile past Scotts Road on the left is the Settlers Monument Path.)
- Continue on North Sea Road under the railroad tracks to the merge with Main Street. Continue on Main to the ride starting point in the village parking lot.

Beach is the beginning of a 2-mile-long run along Southampton Beach. The road ends at Shinnecock Inlet, with a great view of Shinnecock Bay to the north. All along this road are spectacular beach dwellings for which Southampton is known. From the beach road we head north through additional comfortable and pleasant streets, finally reaching Hill Street (Route 27A). We go west on Hill Street past the Shinnecock Indian reservation on the left, where cyclists are not welcome, to Tuckahoe Road. We proceed north on Tuckahoe through Southampton College, then over the railroad tracks to Route 27 (marked Route 39). Next we proceed across this road with care (the two-way traffic is usually extremely heavy) and then through the Shinnecock Hills Golf Club, to the beginning of a run through the hillier and more wooded sections of North Sea. At the end of Barker Isle Road is Bullhead Bay, an attractive sheltered inlet usually harboring a number of small boats, from which we proceed 2 1/2 miles through hilly pleasant country. The road is lined with stands of oak covered in places with shrouds of cat briar. There are very few homes in the area so that it is one of those increasingly rare stretches where natural Long Island vegetation can be viewed quietly, close-up, and in some abundance. At its end we come to North Sea Road, where we head north to Conscience Point. A road marker indicates the way to the landing site of the original Southampton settlers. A plaque on a large boulder at water's edge commemorates the event. At the end of North Sea Road is a beach at which swimming is allowed but at which no amenities are provided. The view, however, is striking looking out over Peconic Bay to Robins Island on the left and Little Hog Neck on the north fork directly opposite. We return to Southampton on North Sea Road, which is rather unspectacular and also has some traffic.

There are several interesting historical sights in the village that might be of interest after the ride. These include the Elias Pelletreau Silver Shop (c. 1750) on Main Street near Cameron Street; the Southampton Historical Museum at Main and Meeting House Lane; the Halsey House Museum (c. 1650) on South Main Street; and Hollyhocks (c. 1650) at Main and Foster streets.

27. Bridgehampton — Water Mill

Number of miles: 20 (12 miles for short ride through Bridgehampton)
Approximate pedaling time: 4 hours (short ride 2 hours)
Terrain: Flat
Surface: Good; sandy in places
Traffic: Light
Things to see: Berwind Memorial, Hedges Homestead, Water Mill Village Green, Old Water Mill Museum, Bridgehampton Historical Museum

Halfway between Southampton and Easthampton lies Bridgehampton, and a few miles west of it, the village of Water Mill. In the hierarchy of vacation spots on Long Island's south fork, Bridgehampton rates somewhere between those venerable communities and Westhampton and Hampton Bays. Bridgehampton differs from others, however, in that it seems to have an identity independent of its summer-resort image. Just a short distance from the village center are open, rich farmlands that surround the community, stretching south to the ocean beaches and north to the center of the peninsula. While Bridgehampton has its share of expensive summer housing, a closer look finds it to be a prosperous farming area. This ride tours both the farms and the playgrounds and some of the interesting historical sights along the way.

The ride starts from the village center and proceeds south on Ocean Road to Sagaponack Road, past the Berwind Memorial, a windmill built around 1830 and moved several times before arriving at its present location. We head west on Sagaponack and once past the Bridgehampton Golf Club come to the beginning of farmland. The farms have been altered at their edges somewhat by the building of year-round homes, which themselves appear quite substantial. This pattern of farms and new homes exists throughout the area south of the village.

After crossing over Sagaponack Lake, a beautiful narrow sheet of calm water, we turn south at Ocean Road. On the right at the Bridge Lane-Ocean Road intersection is the Hedges Homestead, built in the mid-1700s. At Mecox Road we follow the signs to the town beaches. Heading out on Jobs Lane we see the first of the

How to get there: East on Route 27 to the village of Bridgehampton. Park in the municipal parking lot on the south side of Route 27 opposite the public library, just west of the Veteran's Monument.

DIRECTIONS FOR THE RIDE:

- Go right from the parking lot on Route 27 to Ocean Road at the Veteran's Monument.
- Right on Ocean Road, past the Berwind Memorial Park, to Sagaponack Road on the left.
- Left on Sagaponack Road past the Bridgehampton Golf Club about 1 1/2 miles to Main Street.
- Right at Main Street about 1 mile to Bridge Lane.
- Right on Bridge Lane, over Sagaponack Lake Bridge, to Ocean Road. Hedges Homestead is on the right.
- Left on Ocean Road about 1 mile to Mecox Road.
- Right on Mecox 1/4 mile to Jobs Lane on the left.
- Left on Jobs Lane to its end at Mecox Beach, then right on Dune Road to Westcott-Cameron Beach, a distance of about 2 miles. Return on Dune Road and Jobs Lane to Mecox Road.
- Left on Mecox Road for about 2 miles (bearing right at Bay Lane 1/4 mile along) to Route 27 (Montauk Highway). Those wishing to return to Bridgehampton can go right on Paul's Lane, the first right past Bay Lane, then right at the unmarked intersection to Halsey Lane on the left. Go left on Halsey Lane to Hildreth Lane, then right to Ocean Road, the left back to Montauk Highway (Route 27).
- Left on Route 27 about 1/2 mile to Rose Hill Road on the left.
- Left on Rose Hill Road about 1 mile to its end at Mecox Bay.
- From Mecox Bay go left on Halsey Lane for about 1 mile to Route 27 at the windmill.
- Jog left on Route 27 to Old Mill Road on the right.
- Right on Old Mill Road, with the Old Water Mill Museum on the left, over the railroad tracks to Upper Seven Ponds Road.
- Left on Upper Seven Ponds Road to Head of Pond Road.
- Right on Head of Pond Road for about 3 miles (going left at Deerfield Lane) to the merge with Scuttlehole Road at Strongs Lane.
- Go left on Scuttlehole Road for about 1 1/2 miles, past the ponds to Mitchell Lane.
- Right on Mitchell Lane about 1 1/2 miles to the merge with Butter Lane at the railroad overpass, then continue right on Butter Lane under the overpass to Route 27.
- Left on Route 27, with the Bridgehampton Historical Museum on the left, about 1/2 mile to the ride starting point.

modern beach-home architecture common in the wealthier sections of the south fork. In contrast to the older-style homes of dark cedar bordered with white trim, these are stark and gaunt, in pale shades of gray with flashes of glass and plastic. They are located in unprotected open sand stretches and knolls, appearing somewhat forlorn in their sleek efficiency.

At the end of Jobs Lane we come to Mecox Beach on the open Atlantic. Just over the high dunes can be seen the crashing breakers of the ocean, white froth on pale green water — a great sight. A mile or so further along on Dune Road is Westcott-Cameron Beach, another opening to the Atlantic. The ride out and back to Wescott provides an excellent view of more beach homes and Mecox Bay and Water Mill to the north. Refreshments and rest rooms are available at the pavilion on the dunes.

From the beaches we head north on Mecox Road through 2 miles or so of tranquil farms and homes, at the end of which is Montauk Highway (Route 27). The next 1/2 mile requires riding on the shoulder of this heavily trafficked road, but at Rose Hill Road we enter peaceful farm country once again at Water Mill. At the end of Rose Hill Road is an opening to Mecox Bay, providing an excellent view of that body, and in the distance the beach dunes we previously cycled past. At the end of Halsey Lane we come again to Montauk Highway at the Water Mill village green, with its windmill landmark built around 1800.

The shops along Montauk Highway have been remodeled in the manner of a colonial village and are quite attractive. We proceed over Montauk Highway onto Upper Seven Ponds Road to the Old Water Mill Museum. This mill was built in 1644 and has been restored so that it can once again grind the corn and grains grown in the area. Power is supplied as it always has been by the quiet flow from Mill Pond just north of the museum. Demonstrations of grinding are given every day. In addition there are displays of tools and instruments used by the early settlers and colonists.

The remainder of the ride goes through 5 miles of productive farmland, a great deal of it grass sod that will end up on the lawns of Nassau County. As we return to the center of the village and the ride starting point we pass on the left the Bridgehampton Historical Museum, housed in the August Corwith Homestead, built around 1770.

28. Sag Harbor — North Haven

Number of miles: 13
Approximate pedaling time: 2 hours
Terrain: Hilly
Surface: Good; rough in some places
Traffic: Heavy
Things to see: Shelter Island Ferry landing, Foster Memorial
 Beach, Sag Harbor Whaling Museum, Whalers Church

Sag Harbor was Long Island's center of whaling for half a century during the early and mid-1800s. After a crude start on the beaches of Southampton and Easthampton, where whales often beached and were thus easily taken, residents of Long Island's eastern end went to sea from Sag Harbor and joined the great American whaling fleet. With Nantucket, New Bedford, and New London, Sag Harbor prospered from the lucrative whale hunts. It is estimated that as many as sixty whaling vessels were based in Sag Harbor in 1847, at the zenith of the town's whaling activity. With the coming of petroleum-based oil, however, the demand for whale oil gradually dwindled, as did the fortunes of Sag Harbor. The last whaling ship left port in 1874.

This heritage is both tangible and visible in the setting, architecture, and nautical atmosphere of the village. Overlaying it all is the ambience of a summer recreation center — much like its counterpart villages on the south shore and the eastern end of the north fork. Sag Harbor offers, in addition to its exceptionally scenic location, a variety of restaurants, bookstores, antique shops, and other attractions that make it a perfect place to end a day's riding.

The ride starts on Main Street and proceeds north from the village. At the base of Main Street we cross the bridge to North Haven and view along the way Gardiners Bay to the east and Sag Harbor Cove to the west. It was these sheltered bodies of water that provided safe harbor for the whalers, who were away for long periods of time — often for three years or more.

The ride traverses North Haven along Ferry Road for a distance of about 3 miles through a pleasant area of established and well-tended homes. At the end of Ferry Road can be seen the

How to get there: East on Route 27 to Bridge-hampton, then north on Route 79 to Sag Harbor. Park in the municipal parking lot at Spring and Main streets.

DIRECTIONS FOR THE RIDE:

- From the parking lot at Spring and Main streets, go left on Main to Long Wharf and the Windmill.
- Proceed right onto Route 114 (Ferry Road) over the bridge to North Haven. Continue on Ferry Road for about 3 miles to its end at the Shelter Island ferry landing. Those wishing to ride on Shelter Island can use the Shelter Island directions (Ride 16).
- Return on Route 114 about 1 1/4 miles to the Sunset Beach Road turnoff to the right at the "114 South" sign.
- Continue on Sunset Beach Road for about 1 mile to its end at Noyack Bay.
- Return on Sunset Beach Road one block to Tyndall Road on the right.
- Right on Tyndall Raod to Short Beach Road, to the right at the Route 114 intersection.
- Right at Short Beach Road for about 2 miles along Noyack Bay, past Foster Memorial Beach, to the end of the road at the Noyack Road (Route 38) intersection. The Salty Dog Restaurant is on the right.
- Left on Noyack Road, continuing onto Stony Hill Road for about 1 3/4 miles to Brick Kiln Road.
- Left on Brick Kiln Road, past Hildreth Street, to Main Street at Mashashimuet Park.
- Left on Main Street for about 1 mile to the ride starting point.

Shelter Island ferries, small open-ended boats that constantly ply the narrow crossing. (The ferry landing on Shelter Island is a terminal point for the Shelter Island bike ride described in Ride 16.)

We return from the ferry landing along Ferry Road for a short distance to Sunset Beach Road, which runs for about a mile to Noyack Bay. This is an exceptionally pleasant leg, passing through a quiet, tree-lined area and ending at a small, pebbly beach providing a terrific view of the bay.

The next leg of the ride, on Short Beach Road, follows the bay shoreline along Foster Memorial Beach, an easy 2-mile run that offers an excellent view of the bay and a opportunity fir swimming. At the end of Short Beach Road is the Salty Dog Restaurant, a landmark establishment, and on the left, a historical marker describing a Revolutionary War skirmish that occurred at the site.

The ride turns south on Noyack Road at this point and begins the return to the village. The riding is more difficult from here on because of the more challenging terrain. Noyack Road itself has narrow shoulders and presents a fairly steep hill climb. Some auto traffic can be expected as well. At Brick Kiln Road, however, where the ride turns left, a long downhill run begins that takes us back into the village center. Along Brick Kiln Road are large modern houses that contrast sharply with the historic architecture of the village. The ride turns left on Main Street at Masashimuet Park, with its striking veterans' monument, for a 1-mile run to the starting point.

The Sag Harbor village center is a National Historic District and boasts dozens of architectural gems, some of which date from colonial times. A guide to the village that details twenty-five distinctive structures can be obtained from the Chamber of Commerce office in the windmill at the foot of Main Street. Of special interest are the Sag Harbor Whaling Museum (c. 1850), a Greek Revival structure at Main and Garden streets, known for its collection of whaling artifacts and nautical histories; and the Whaler's Church (c. 1840), an outstanding example in wood of Egyptian Revival architecture.

29. East Hampton—Amagansett

Number of miles: 17 (29 with Springs-Fireplace loop)
Approximate pedaling time: 3 hours (7 with Springs-Fireplace loop)
Terrain: Flat in East Hampton-Amagansett, some hills in Springs-Fireplace
Surface: Good; sandy in places
Traffic: Heavy on Main Street, East Hampton, light elsewhere
Things to see: East Hampton Town Marine Museum, Beach Hampton, Gerard Drive peninsula on Gardiners Bay

The village of East Hampton is the easternmost of the Hampton communities of the south fork. It is an old and extremely attractive place rich in historical sights, enhanced with a location on the open Atlantic. In addition to the beachfront, the community contains a number of attractive ponds and lakes and is surrounded in part by pleasant expanses of farms. To the north is a hillier area, mostly tree-covered, with here and there a small farm, that runs to Gardiners Bay, along which are numerous ragged and irregular small inlets and harbors.

The ride consists of two segments: the basic ride, running through East Hampton, Amagansett, and the Atlantic beaches, and a northern loop running to Gardiners Bay through the communities of Springs and Fireplace. The northern loop more than doubles the length of the ride and goes through a moderately hilly area, but for those up to it, it makes an excellent whole-day bicycling outing.

The ride begins from the eastern end of East Hampton Village and proceeds south toward the beach on Egypt Lane. Along this road are typical summer homes for which East Hampton is famous — luxurious mansions of weathered cedar on large manicured lawns shaded by tall graceful trees. At the end of Egypt Lane is the Maidstone Club, dating from the late 1800s, with its open vistas of clipped fairways. We proceed east from here along Further Lane for about 2 miles, through an area of farms and pleasant homes to Indian Wells Road, where we turn south to the beach. The ocean air is exhilarating and the surf enticing on hot days. For contrast, try to imagine earlier times on the beach when East Hampton colonists worked its dunes searching for beached whales, which were cut and tried right there, a profitable and common occurrence then.

We return from the beach on Indian Wells Road and continue east on Bluff Road. From here we get a panoramic view of the grass-covered dunes and several small homes standing forlornly on them. Opposite Hand Lane, on the right, is the East Hampton Town Marine Museum, featuring displays of south-fork fishing processes and whaling history. We turn north at Atlantic Avenue, but it might be of interest to observe the community of Beach Hampton about a mile or so further east on the beach, to see the results of modern beachfront development. The expensive and ultramodern beach-homes are jammed so closely together that a claustrophobic quality is created that completely destroys the open beach atmosphere that most people come here for. It is a congested suburban cluster at the ocean's edge, startlingly different from the older East Hampton.

We proceed north on Atlantic Avenue to Main Street, Amagansett, then right over the railroad tracks, entering farm country at Stone Highway. Here and along Town Lane back to East Hampton we are in the argricultural working land of the area. While there are some summer residences, most of the land is devoted to farming or is undeveloped. We turn south from Town Lane on Old Acabonack Road, proceed through a neighborhood of small homes and commercial establishments, and arrive back on Pantigo Lane-Main Street in East Hampton.

East Hampton dates from 1648 when the first English settlers arrived from Massachusetts. After purchasing the land from the Montauk Indians, at a bargain price in clothing and tools (valued at the time at about thirty pounds, the annual pay of a schoolmaster), they formed a close-knit, industrious Puritan community. They thrived on farming and fishing but remained secluded and distant until the charms of the village were noticed by those wealthy individuals of the mid-1800s who had the wherewithal to travel this far to escape the heat and dust of New York City in summer. The village became a center for wealthy summer vacationists and remained an exclusive and remote compound until the railroad and improved road system reached it at the turn of the century. Even then it remained a place for more well-to-do vacationers. The village still displays an air of substance with its broad and opulent main streets with large homes, expensive shops, and tanned, well-dressed pedestrians.

Along Main Street are several well-preserved historical structures and homes. At the east end is the Old Hook mill, built in 1806. Further west in the village center along Main Street is the Presbyterian Church, on the left just past Davids Lane, built in 1860. At Dunmere Lane is Guild Hall on the left and Clinton Academy on the right. Guild Hall houses an extensive collection of paintings by artists who at one time lived in East Hampton; Clinton Academy, a restored eighteenth-century school building, displays historical items from East Hampton and its surrounding communities. Further on, on James Lane on the left, is the Mulford House and the Home Sweet Home Museum. Both these buildings date from the seventeenth century, the latter commemorating the composer, John Howard Payne. We continue on past Town Pond where at 217 Main Street can be seen the residence used by President John Tyler during a visit to Long Island in 1845.

We continue west and away from the village center and proceed on Ocean Avenue, Lily Pond Road, and Georgica Avenue through an area of extremely large and fashionable homes. The neighborhood changes abruptly at Montauk Highway where we begin a short leg along Green Hollow and Buckskill roads, through a rural working area. We reenter the village on Woods Lane, where some traffic can be expected, and proceed back on Main Street to the ride starting point.

The northern loop through the communities of Springs and Fireplace provides a pleasant ramble through a very lightly developed area to the north shore of the peninsula on Gardiners Bay. The loop starts at Stone Highway and Town Lane and proceeds north on Old Stone Highway. The road is lined with densely treed sections alternating with small homesites. On Gerard Drive we run to the end of a narrow peninsula that encloses Acabonack Harbor. Out in Gardiners Bay is Gardiners Island, visible to the northeast. The island was purchased from the Montauk Indians by Lyon Gardiner in 1639, becoming the first English settlement in what is now New York State. We proceed from here through Fireplace and then south past Three Mile Harbor. The ride from Three Mile Harbor south to East Hampton runs through a nondescript mix of light woods, small homes, and commercial establishments, with increasing traffic as you approach the village. We rejoin the basic ride route at Pantigo Road and North Main Street.

How to get there: East on Route 27 through Southampton and Bridgehampton, following signs to East Hampton. Park in the municipal parking lot at Park Place on the left off Main or at Fithian Lane, right off Main.

DIRECTIONS FOR THE RIDE:

- Go east from the parking lot on Main Street toward the windmill to Egypt Lane on the right.
- Right on Egypt Lane about 1 mile to its end, at the Maidstone Golf Club, then left at Dunmere onto Further Lane.
- Proceed on Further Lane for about 2 1/4 miles, past the merge with Skimhampton Road to Indian Wells Highway.
- Right on Indian Wells to its end at Indian Wells Beach.
- From the beach go right on Bluff Road past the East Hampton Town Marine Museum, about 3/4 mile, to Atlantic Avenue. (Beach Hampton, about a mile east of here, can be entered at Mako Road.)
- Left on Atlantic Avenue about 3/4 mile to Montauk Highway (Route 27).
- Right on Montauk Highway for one block, bearing left over the railroad tracks to Stone Highway on the left.
- Left on Stone Highway about 3/4 mile to Town Lane on the left.
- Left on Town Lane for about 2 1/4 miles to Acabonack Road. (The Springs-Fireplace Loop starts here; see directions below.)
- Left on Acabonack Road for about 1 mile; then bear left under the railroad overpass to Pantigo Road. (The Springs-Fireplace Loop rejoins the basic ride here.)
- Right on Pantigo Road (Main Street) past the ride starting point about 1 1/4 miles through the village of East Hampton to Ocean Avenue, across the intersection at which Route 27 turns right.
- Continue on Ocean Avenue for about 3/4 mile to Lily Pond Lane on the right.
- Right on Lily Pond Lane for about 1 1/2 miles to Apaquogue Road.
- Right on Apaquogue Road to La Forest Lane on the left.
- Left on La Forest to its end at Georgica Road.
- Left on Georgica Road past Georgica Cove about 3/4 mile to Montauk Highway (Route 27), going right at the fork.
- Proceed over Route 27, jogging left onto Green Hollow Road, then continue on for 1/2 mile to Buckskill Road.
- Right on Buckskill Road for about 3/4 mile over Route 27, to its end at Baiting Hollow Road.
- Right on Baiting Hollow Road for 1/2 mile to Georgica Road.
- Left on Georgica Road about 3/4 mile to Woods Lane, Route 27.

- Right on Woods Lane, following Route 27 west through the village to the ride starting point on Main Street.

Springs-Fireplace Loop:
- From Stone Highway at Town Lane, proceed right on Springs-Old Stone Highway Road.
- Continue on Springs-Old Stone Highway for 2 1/2 miles to Neck Path.
- Right at Neck Path, continuing on Old Stone Highway past Acabonack Road, for about 1 mile to Springs-Fireplace Road.
- Right on Springs-Fireplace Road about 1 3/4 miles to Gerard Drive on the right.
- Right on Gerard Drive for about a 3-mile round-trip on Gerard Peninsula, enclosing Acabonack Harbor.
- Go right from Gerard Drive on Old Fireplace Road to Hog Creek Lane.
- Left on Hog Creek Lane about 1/2 mile to Kings Point Road.
- Left on Kings Point Road about 3/4 mile to Hog Creek Road.
- Right on Hog Creek Road, which becomes Three Mile Harbor Road, for about 5 1/4 miles to the merge with North Main Street in East Hampton village.
- Continue on North Main Street, under the railroad overpass to Pantigo Road. Follow the basic ride from here.

30. Montauk

Number of miles: 17 (25 with Hither Hills State Park Loop)
Approximate pedaling time: 4 hours (6 hours with Hither Hills Loop)
Terrain: Moderately hilly
Surface: Good; sandy in places
Traffic: Heavy in Montauk, moderate elsewhere
Things to see: Montauk Point Lighthouse, Oyster Pond overlook, Star Island, Hither Hills State Park

Montauk is the easternmost extremity of the south fork, reaching 120 miles into the Atlantic from New York City. It is a narrow peninsula, hilly in places, with a constant sea breeze and clear, clean air. The Atlantic beats along its beaches on its southern edge, and Block Island Sound intrudes in several bays and inlets along its north shore. Its developed areas include Montauk Beach near Hither Hills State Park at the western end and Montauk village and Ditch Plains near its center. The eastern end, unpopulated, is devoted to state and county park use, a small Air Force radar station, and, at the very tip of the peninsula, the famous Montauk Point lighthouse station.

We proceed east from the village center on Montauk Point State Parkway (Route 27) toward Montauk Point. This road can have appreciable traffic, but the shoulder is wide and smooth and the hills long and gentle. Once past the populated sections of Ditch Plains and Lake Montauk, we come to the open country that once served as a grazing area for great herds of cattle. Every year they were brought in from western Long Island for fattening. The cattle were tended by individuals, appointed by the company that owned the land, who lived in the only three houses on the peninsula. Third House, the most easterly of the three, on the left just past East Lake Drive and Deep Hollow Ranch, was built in 1806, replacing a structure built in 1749. In 1898 Third House and the surrounding fields were used as a quarantine area for Theodore Roosevelt and 30,000 other U.S. Army troops just returned from the Spanish-American War.

About a mile along on the right is an overlook from which you get a good view of the hills of the point, Oyster Pond across the way, and Block Island Sound with Rhode Island in the distance. At

MONTAUK POINT
MONTAUK STATE PARK
STATE PARKWAY
LIGHTHOUSE
MONTAUK A.F. STATION
OYSTER POND
DEEP OVERLOOK
MONTAUK PARK (SUF. CO.)
THIRD HOUSE
THEODORE ROOSEVELT CO. PARK
BIG REED POND
EAST LAKE DRIVE
STATE ISLAND
LAKE MONTAUK
MONTAUK PT. HOLLOW RANCH
27
MONTAUK
INLET
SOUND VIEW
27
WEST LAKE DRIVE
DITCH PLAINS RD.
OCEAN
MONTAUK MANOR
FLAMINGO AVE.
OFFICE TOWER
FORT POND
GROSBY SECOND HOUSE
EDGEMERE
START HERE
MONTAUK HIGHWAY
SECOND HOUSE
MONTAUK BEACH
OLD MONTAUK HIGHWAY
HITHER HILLS STATE PARK
CAMPING BEACH
BLOCK ISLAND SOUND
ATLANTIC OCEAN
N
1 MILE
1/2
0

How to get there: East on Route 27 through
Bridgehampton and East Hampton to the village of
Montauk. Park in the public parking lot on Edgemere
and South Euclid streets, near the tall office (condominium) building.

DIRECTIONS FOR THE RIDE:

- From the parking lot at Edgemere and South Euclid streets, proceed left to Montauk Point State Parkway (Route 27), then left again for about 5 1/2 miles past Third House and the overlook to Montauk Point and the lighthouse.
- Return on Route 27 about 4 1/2 miles to Ditch Plains Road on the left.
- Left on Ditch Plains Road for about 1/2 mile to the beach and back.
- Go left on Route 27 1/4 mile to West Lake Drive (Route 77) on the right.
- Right on West Lake Drive about 1 3/4 miles to Star Island turnoff.
- Right onto Star Island and return.
- Continue north on West Lake Drive to the Lake Montauk inlet parking area.
- From the inlet proceed south on Route 49 (Flamingo Avenue) 3 1/2 miles, past Montauk Manor, onto Edgemere Road. Continue to the ride starting point at South Euclid Street.

Hither Hills State Park Loop:

- Proceed west from the ride starting point about 1/2 mile on Route 27 (Montauk Highway) to the Old Montauk Highway turnoff on the left, just past Second House Museum.
- Continue on Old Montauk Highway for about 3 1/2 miles to Hither Hills State Park camping and swimming beach.
- Return on Old Montauk Highway or on Route 27 (Montauk Highway).

to end of Route 27 is Montauk Point State Park and the lighthouse. The lighthouse stands 100 feet tall on a cliff on Turtle Cove, putting the light 170 feet above sea level. There are, of course, excellent views of the turbulent race where the waters of the Atlantic and Block Island Sound meet east of the point. The lighthouse, built in 1795, was originally placed about 300 feet from the cliff edge. Since that time the ocean has eaten away at the point to the extent that it is almost lapping at the foundations of the light. In time, no doubt, the light will have to be moved inland.

We return to Montauk with a short diversion to the beach at Ditch Plains, a small community of beach homes, and then proceed north on West Lake Drive. About 2 miles along on the right is the Star Island turnoff, from which you get a good view of Lake Montauk and its inlet on Block Island Sound. We continue north to the inlet itself where we find the major industry of Montauk: the fishermen, commercial and recreational, who can be seen going through the inlet in a continuous parade of boats of all kinds. The neighborhood abounds in restaurants, fish dealers, marinas, and boatyards. There is no more briny place in all Long Island.

Proceeding south from the inlet, about halfway along on Flamingo Road we pass the eastern terminus of the Long Island Railroad. On the left at the top of a hill is Montauk Manor, which, with the tall office tower (now a residential condominium complex) in the center of the village, is the remains of an ill-fated attempt to develop Montauk as the "Miami of the north" in the 1920s. Swimming beaches are located near the village center on South Edgewater Avenue, running for several blocks on the Atlantic.

We proceed west from the village center on Route 27 for a loop through Hither Hills State Park. We pass Second House Museum, built in 1746, on the right at Second House Road, and we turn left just past this onto Old Montauk Highway. This is a curving, undulating, bumpy road that provides an excellent view of the ocean and the many attractive vacation homes built along its edge in the community of Montauk Beach. At its end is the picnic, swimming, and camping area of the park. Hither Hills consists of 1,755 acres, most of it in the woodlands to the north. You can cycle through these beautiful stretches of oak by returning to Montauk on Route 27.

Appendix:
Traffic-Free Rides in
Nassau and Western Suffolk

All the rides presented in this book use public roads, thereby requiring the cyclist to have some confidence and familiarity with bicycling in traffic. Those just learning to ride, regaining their bicycling legs, or riding with young children might be interested in practicing first on the traffic-free bike paths listed below.

1. Wantagh Parkway—Jones Beach Bikeway.

Bordering Wantagh Parkway from Merrick Road south to the Marine Theater parking lot at Jones Beach.

A 4 1/2-mile bike path starting at Cedar Creek Park, 1/4 mile east of Wantagh Parkway on Merrick Road, traverses a number of bays and marshes on the way to the beach. There are three bridges with excellent water views. Cycling is not allowed at Jones Beach itself, however, so to visit the beach your bike must be left in a corral at the end of the bikeway. Lock your bike, then walk the 1/2 mile to the beach.

2. Eisenhower Park (Nassau County).

Just east of Meadowbrook Parkway in East Meadow.

Four miles of paths go by ball fields, playgrounds, picnic areas, and past a golf course and pond. This is the best all-around traffic-free ride on Long Island.

3. Wantagh Park (Nassau County).

West side of Wantagh Parkway, south of Merrick Road.

About 2 miles of paths pass by playgrounds and ball fields, with attractive bay and harbor views.

4. Bethpage State Parkway.

Massapequa Preserve.

A paved path runs south from Bethpage State Park for nearly 2 miles along Bethpage State Parkway, then continues for another 2 miles on a packed dirt road through the preserve. The road parallels a pleasant stream and several small ponds.

5. Long Beach Boardwalk.

On the ocean in Long Beach.

This 2-mile, planked boardwalk affords an expansive ocean view. The boardwalk is lined with hotels and vacation homes and attracts a good number of pedestrians and joggers. Unfortunately, cycling is not allowed from noon to 6 P.M. on Saturdays, Sundays, or holidays during the summer.

6. Caumsett State Park.
Lloyd Neck, Huntington.

Four miles of paths through the 1,500-acre former Marshall Field Estate overlooking Long Island Sound. Exceptionally scenic grounds and water views.

7. Valley Stream State Park.
Between Exits 14 and 15 on the Southern State Parkway at Valley Stream.

Three miles of paths with other amenities typical of the state parks on Long Island, with picnicking, ball fields, and children's play areas. Paths generally run through wooded areas.

8. Hempstead Lake State Park.
Exit 18 on the Southern State Parkway in Hempstead.

A 2-mile path along Hempstead Lake and Peninsula Boulevard passes through a pleasant wooded area.

9. Belmont Lake State Park.
Exits 37 and 38 on the Southern State Parkway in Babylon.

Three miles of paths encircle Belmont Lake through picnic areas, ball fields, and woods.

10. Sunken Meadow State Park.
At the end of Sunken Meadow State Parkway in Smithtown.

Three miles of paths through open fields end at a bathing beach on Long Island Sound.

11. Heckscher State Park.
At the end of Heckscher State Parkway in Islip.

Two miles of paths through ball fields, picnic areas, and woods lead to a bathing beach on Great South Bay.

Short Bike Rides, Best Bike Rides, and Short Nature Walks Series

Short Bike Rides in Eastern Massachusetts, $12.95

Short Bike Rides in Central and Western Massachusetts, $9.95

Short Bike Rides in Eastern Pennsylvania, $8.95

Short Bike Rides in Rhode Island, $9.95

Short Bike Rides on Cape Cod, Nantucket, and the Vineyard, $8.95

Short Bike Rides in Connecticut, $8.95

Short Bike Rides on Long Island, $8.95

Short Bike Rides in New Jersey, $8.95

Short Bike Rides in and around Washington, D.C., $9.95

Short Bike Rides in and around New York City, $9.95

Short Bike Rides in and around Los Angeles, $11.95

Short Bike Rides in Western Washington, $12.95

Short Bike Rides in and around Philadelphia, $9.95

The Best Bike Rides in New England, $12.95

The Best Bike Rides in the Pacific Northwest, $12.95

The Best Bike Rides in the South, $12.95

The Best Bike Rides in the Midwest, $12.95

The Best Bike Rides in the Mid-Atlantic, $12.95

Short Nature Walks on Long Island, $8.95

Short Nature Walks on Cape Cod and the Vineyard, $8.95

Sixty Selected Short Nature Walks in Connecticut, $8.95

To order any of these titles with Mastercard or Visa, call toll-free 1–800–243–0495; in Connecticut call 1–800–962–0973. Free shipping for orders of three or more books. Connecticut residents add sales tax. Ask for your free catalogue of Globe Pequot's quality books on recreation, travel, nature, gardening, cooking, crafts, and more. Prices and availability subject to change.